A KNIGHT IN BATTLE

By the same author:
A KNIGHT AND HIS ARMOR
A KNIGHT AND HIS HORSE
A KNIGHT AND HIS CASTLE
A KNIGHT AND HIS WEAPONS
DARK AGE WARRIOR
THE ARCHAEOLOGY OF WEAPONS
THE SWORD IN THE AGE OF CHIVALRY

About the Author

Ewart Oakeshott was born in 1916. He began collecting swords while still in school at Dulwich, and has since built up a superb collection, specializing in the medieval period. His books include *The Archaeology of Weapons, European Weapons and Armour, The Sword in the Age of Chivalry,* and the acclaimed "Knight" series. He always brings to his books a wide and deep knowledge of his subject, and a witty and pithy style. The *Times Educational Supplement* rightly called him "one of those rarely gifted researchers who combine exhaustive investigation with absorbing enthusiasm." Oakeshott (and three friends) founded the Arms and Armour Society, a concern with a worldwide membership. His home is in Ely, close to Cambridge, England.

A KNIGHT IN BATTLE

Second Edition

EWART OAKESHOTT F.S.A.
Illustrated by the author

Dufour Editions

1971,
this revised second edition published 1998

Published in the United States of America by
Dufour Editions Inc.,
Chester Springs, Pennsylvania 19425

Library of Congress Cataloging-in-Publication Data

Oakeshott, R. Ewart.
    A knight in battle / Ewart Oakeshott ; illustrated
by the author. – 2nd ed.
        p.   cm.
    Includes bibliographical references and index.
    ISBN 0-8023-1322-1
    1. Weapons–Europe–History. 2. Armor, Medieval–History.
3. Military art and science–History–Medieval, 500-1500.
4. Military history, Medieval. 5. Knights and knighthood.
I. Title.
U810.01724   1997
623.4.41–dc21   97-36071
                                                           CIP

ISBN 0-8023-1322-1

Printed and bound in the
United States of America

Contents

Introduction

Many people imagine that medieval battles were all alike, with similar tactics and fighting styles. But the truth is deeper, more complex, and revealing. During a period roughly between the years 1100 A.D. and 1500, there were countless battles, big and small, waged all over Europe and the Middle East, all quite different from each other. Take any medieval period, say the first twenty years of the thirteenth century, and you will find that all the battles fought during that time differed. Weapons and armor occasionally might be the same, but the tactical style of each fight would not be. So when spanning the four centuries of "the age of chivalry," we are bound to find great variation in tactical fighting methods – and in armaments too.

In this book I describe four battles in order to show some of these variations; I have chosen little-known battles because well-known ones such as Hastings, Lewes, Crécy, Agincourt, and Barnet have been described so many times before. I doubt if more than a few readers have ever heard of the battles at Arsuf (1191), Lincoln (1217), Mauron (1352), and Marignano (1515), but each one illustrates a different style of fighting.

During this period, great changes took place in the weapons used in war, and these changes affected the way armies were raised and trained, battles fought, and wars conducted. Until the end of the thirteenth century, these changes were merely of detail and not of military significance. But from 1280 onward, the perpetual conflict between weapons of offense and methods of defense began to be decided more and more in favor of the offensive weapon. And then, with the coming of extremely effective and reliable small guns that could be carried and handled by individual men and shot accurately and repeatedly over reasonably long distances, the day of the armored horseman was over for good. But the change came slowly, for before the invention of any kind of gun a missile weapon of terrible power and rapidity of shooting changed the whole concept of war in western Europe.

Arrow piles. These are unlike the traditionally accepted form of arrowhead, the sharp cutting edges of the piles being no broader than the actual shaft of the arrow. In this way there was nothing to stop the deep penetration of the arrow.

This missile weapon was the longbow in the practiced hands of English yeomen during the fourteenth century. But the weapon was Welsh in origin. It was the weapon of the men of Gwent, and from Anglo-Saxon times the English had known it and dreaded it in that area of constant war between Wales and England, the long stretch of the "March" between the two countries running north to south between Chester and Monmouth.

What made the Welsh longbow such a terrible weapon was the penetrating power of its arrows and the rapidity with which the archer could shoot them off – five aimed shots in a minute. The arrows could pierce the armor of even the best-protected knight. Keep in mind that this period was before plate armor came into use, so even the wealthiest knight had to rely mainly on mail. Historian Gerald of Wales, writing in the late twelfth century of the events taking place in the Welsh borderlands during his lifetime, tells a story of a patrol of English men-at-arms ambushed by Welsh bowmen in 1188. He noticed how one man-at-arms was pinned to his horse by an arrow that pierced not only the skirt of his mail hauberk, but also the padded gambeson beneath it. The arrow then went through both the mail hose on the man's thigh and the thigh itself, and then out again through the mail on the inside of the leg, through the wood and leather of the saddle, and finally into the horse. When the man wheeled around to try to escape, the bowman got him in the same way in the other leg. Gerald also tells of a sight he saw at Abergavenny Castle: four arrows sticking into an oak door, with the points – or piles as they were called – standing an inch or more clear of the wood inside the door. And to think: the door was made of oak planks two inches thick. The garrison of the castle, so tickled by these arrows shot by Welsh besiegers four years or so before Gerald saw them, left them in the door as a souvenir.

Despite its awfully destructive power, this form of bow and arrow was fairly unknown elsewhere in England, let alone on the Continent. But Edward I of England, during his campaign in the 1280s to conquer the independent principality of Wales, noticed its military value (or his captains did) and proceeded to arm his own English with it and train them in its use. But the English did not fight with the longbow in the Welsh way, as guerillas in small bands shooting from cover. Instead the Englsh fought as disciplined solid masses of men all shooting together, pouring out volleys of arrows, hundreds at a time. When you have, say, 500 skilled marksmen standing shoulder to shoulder, all shooting together and each man shooting five shafts in a minute, you can see how effective and desperately deadly this fight tactic was. Just imagine 500 arrows in flight at once, followed by waves of 500 more at 12-second intervals. The first wave would be arriving at its target when the last wave left the bows. English bowmen could keep this volley coming as long as they didn't run out of arrows. With this approach and this weapon, the whole concept of war was indeed changing.

Edward I began to use this method against the Scots. But his son Edward II, who was no warrior, had no interest in maintaining this fight style and so did not ensure that a new generation of men received such training; but Edward II's son, Edward III, was a different sort of king altogether. From the start of his reign in 1327 – when he was only fifteen – he set about raising and training a first-class force of bowmen. He raised this force, a sort of territorial army, from the English countryside, finding his men in farms and cottages all over the land. He used them first, and to much success, against the Scots in 1331 and 1333. But still the military minds on the Continent, confident in the overwhelming power of their knightly class, took no warning from Edward III's victories in the North. Then, on a stormy summer evening in 1346, on the bare downs of Ponthieu in northern France near the village of Crécy, a great host of French knights and men-at-arms, the best-armed force in Europe, was swept away in ruin by some 6,000 English archers. Consisting mostly of farmers and laborers, this band of English archers was backed by seven hundred to eight hundred English knights during some 90 minutes of fighting. Not a terribly long stretch of time for a battle, by modern standards, and yet 5,542 French knights lay dead despite their up-to-date equipment and splendid armor.

From that point, it was impossible not to notice the coming of a new weapon. Its immediate effect was the development of a new style of armor, capa-

English bowman, 1360

ble of keeping out even those awful arrows, but the longbow's more far-reaching impact was to alter the style of war. The English archer remained the most dreaded warrior in Europe until, about 100 years after Crécy, he was at last superseded by the hand-gun man, with his horrible little gas-pipe gun and his deadly leaden firepower that no armor could stop.

Even so, heavily armored cavalry remained the backbone of all European armies for nearly 300 years more, and the knights still managed to win victories in spite of the longbow and the gun. The knights who fought with King Francis I of France at Marignano in 1515, for instance, still fought as their crusading ancestors had done, in full armor on horseback with long lances. But the power of these knights was limited not by archers or hand-gun men but by pikemen, both Swiss and Landsknechts.

The pikeman was a professional, non-noble, peasant soldier who fought unarmored in disciplined massed companies, with only the officers and front-rank men wearing light half-armor. Pikemen, as the name implies, fought with pikes, great spears some 15 feet to 18 feet long, weapons almost useless to men fighting individually. But when carried by hundreds of men moving in close formation, these weapons were terribly effective, making an offensive unit capable of crushing all opposition like a bulldozer.

Each man carried a short sword and dagger as well, for close fighting when the company was stuck in the "push of pikes." The Swiss had developed not only this weapon, but also the method of using it, during their long fifteenth-century struggle for independence from the feudal lords of Austria and Bavaria. By the 1480s the Swiss had achieved their purpose, forming an independent state and beginning to earn lots of money by hiring out pikemen to any prince or leader who wanted a good mercenary force. In the long wars that ravaged Italy from 1494 until 1559, Swiss pikemen were constantly employed by the contending great powers – the Holy Roman Empire, the French, the Spanish, and even the pope. Pikemen had one stipulation: if two forces of Swiss were employed on opposing sides, they would not fight each other.

Landsknechts fought in the same manner but were raised in quite a different way. They were not a national force, but a mixed lot of mostly German adventurers who were trained to counter the Swiss. The first armies of Landsknechts were raised in Germany late in the fifteenth century in a deliberate attempt to beat the Swiss at their own game. The Landsknechts were never as good as the Swiss, probably because of a lack of overriding unity.

Although the Swiss bands were mercenaries, each unit was formed from the men of individual cantons – small divisions of territory a bit like English parishes. These men knew each other and were close neighbors in adjoining villages. The Landsknechts companies, on the other hand, comprised a mixed lot of men from all over Europe. They were mainly society's outcasts, often jailbirds given a free pardon for joining. Even so, quite a num-

Landsknecht, 1510. He carries a halberd and wears a short sword of a very distinctive shape (see illustration on page 105). The puffed and slashed clothes he wears became fashionable at the beginning of the 16th century; this was the great age of the mercenary soldier, whose clothes were always getting torn and slashed in fights, in theory if not in practice. Tattered soldiers were fashionable, men's wear followed the fashion, and doublets and hose were made with long cuts in them, with a lining of linen or silk showing through. Even some expensive armor was made in this fashion, imitating the puffs and slashes in embossed steel.

This landsknecht is taken from a drawing made c. 1510 by the German artist Urs Graf. The soldier has only one shoe, and only his left leg wears hose. His right leg is bare, but he has managed to salvage the puffed piece covering the knee. This figure is typical of the tatterdemalion soldier of the period.

ber of landless younger sons of good families joined as well. They were a ferocious and deadly lot, loathed and despised by the Swiss. When Swiss and Landsknechts met in battle, no mercy was shown by either side, whether in dealing with prisoners or the wounded. The Swiss and Landsknechts slaughtered each other with great enthusiasm.

Medieval armies from the eleventh century onward generally were formed in three divisions – or battles, as they were called: vaward, main-battle, and rearward. These names referred to the order in which they marched. Vaward comes from the old English spelling of the French word "avant garde" – vanguard is a variant of it. At any rate, the vaward were at the head of the army, the main-battle in the center, and the rearward in the back. When a force was deployed into battle-order (the word means the process of moving an army from line of march into line of battle), the vaward fell in on the right of the position, the main-battle in the center, and the rearward on the left. These divisions were always maintained as administrative units (like the divisions in a modern army), though on the battlefield they were often split into smaller fighting units or deployed as one great solid mass.

The center was the most honorable command, usually reserved for the monarch or commander-in-chief; next in importance was the right, then the left. The formation of an actual fighting rear-guard, to protect a retreating force, was a different affair. The command of a rear-guard was always a post of great honor, as well as great danger.

In the wars of the sixteenth century the mercenary Landsknecht forces were generally split up so that each of the main divisions of an army had a number of Landsknecht companies, but the Swiss often fought as entire armies. Then they, too, used the three-division system. They went into battle in three columns, or blocks, of men, often five or six thousand men in each, advancing at a steady walk in echelon – that is, with their right-hand column leading, their center a little behind it on its left, and the left-hand column a little behind and to the left of the center. Sometimes they used a large right and center and a small left, and on one or two occasions an enormous right column and a small center and left. Among the pikemen were always a few men with halberds, great axes on long five- or six-foot hafts, and often cantonal banners were defended by a special guard of men with two-handed swords.

An early form of halberd, c. 1320. The blade is about 18 inches from the point of the spike to the lower corner of the blade.

Armies in the twelfth century were raised in an old system that accounts for perhaps their greatest difference from sixteenth-century forces: in the old system, men-at-arms held land on condition that they do military service when called upon by their over-lords. They found their own equipment – horses, arms, armor, baggage, and servants – and received no pay. In the sixteenth century, in its earlier part at least, men-at-arms were called to military service in a somewhat modern way. Though in theory they were called to knight-service by their feudal lords, in practice the system differed from previous times: early sixteenth-century men-at-arms provided their own equipment in the old way, yes, but they were paid for it and got regular monthly pay.

The term "man-at-arms" refers to *any* fighting man who is completely armored and has a horse. He may or may not be a knight. If he were of the knightly class but not a knight, he would be called a squire or sometimes a varlet; but if he were not of knightly rank at all, he would be called a sergeant – what seventy-five years ago in a cavalry regiment would have been known as a trooper.

But it was the infantryman, the poor downtrodden foot-soldier, who saw the greatest change during these four centuries. At the start of this period, foot-soldiers were despised and expendable. They rarely had any measurable effect on a battle, and the infantry of the losing side were always casually slaughtered by the victors. Foot-soldiers were called to battle straight off the land by their lords; ill-equipped, mainly unpaid, often unfed, foot-soldiers were generally a poor lot. Some, however, were professionals. Crossbowmen, for example, needed training to be useful and discipline to be effective; they had to be professionals.

Through the twelfth and thirteenth centuries and into the fourteenth, we find large forces of professional crossbowmen referred to in contemporary writings as "Genoese" or "Flemings." That is because the best companies of these men were raised either in Northern Italy or in the Low Countries. They fought all over Europe and were often hired by crusading princes; we find these crossbowmen engaged in most battles in the period between 1100 and about 1350.

Though professional, tough, and efficient, these hireling soldiers were still utterly despised by the nobility who employed them and by other men-at-arms in general. From about 1350 onward, however, it was different for the English archers, the Swiss, and even the rapscallion Landsknechts. They were respected by their own side, feared by their opponents, and never disdained.

One other thing we have to remember about medieval battles: compared to more recent wars, they engaged few men. The armies of Napoleon commonly had 100,000 or so men; but armies considered large in the Middle Ages had only ten thousand to fifteen thousand men. As for knights, if as many as two hundred took part in a battle, the fighting force would be considered quite strong. It is difficult to work out comparative figures for medieval armies, for contemporary historians and chroniclers of wars and battles before 1500 were generally monks, and most of them seem to have had a poor sense of numbers. They were constantly referring to great hosts of "sixty thousand men" and so on. But we can get a better, more accurate grasp of army sizes by perusing documents extant, in England especially, that give the numbers of men called up for specific campaigns. We have to remember that population was tiny compared with present-day populations. In England today, there are some 57,000,000 people. In 1300 there were less than 3,000,000 altogether. Out of these, of course, only a small proportion would be men of fighting age (between 16 and 60 back then). Few of these men would actually be men-at-arms, and even fewer would be knights. It is doubtful whether the entire knight-service of England came to more than 7,000 at any one time, and it would never have been possible to get every knight in the land called up at once.

Here are a few examples of the numbers of men called up for some English armies. Keep in mind: this is only the number called up; the number who actually showed up would be less, and once the campaign got under way, men dropped out constantly because of sickness and desertion. So even before anyone was wounded or killed in battle, the army would begin shrinking.

At the Battle of Lewes during the Barons' War of 1263-1267, maybe some 11,000 men were engaged on both sides, 4,500 or so on the barons' side and 6,500 on the king's. Of these only a few were knights, for during Henry III's reign there were probably no more than 400 knights available at any one time in all of England and Wales. This doesn't mean there were only 400 knights altogether; only 400 were available for fighting. It has been estimated that in 1277, when Edward I raised his army for his first Welsh campaign, 7,000 knights existed in England, Wales, and Scotland, though only a portion of them would have been available to fight for the king of England. Even so, Edward called on the whole knight-service to come to his banner – and only 375 did.

Sixty-nine years later, in 1346, his grandson Edward III raised the largest English army ever to go over sea; in April of that year 15,000 men mustered at Southampton and Portsmouth. Of these, only 2,000 were men-at-arms and less than half were knights. By the time the battle was fought on August 26, the army was larger because some allied men-at-arms from Gascony were in Edward's force, so there may have been as many as 4,000 men-at-arms present. On the French side the numbers were much greater, though not known for certain. There were probably between 34,000 French and allied troops, plus some 3,500 Genoese mercenary crossbowmen. Of this force, perhaps 8,000 were men-at-arms.

For the 1415 campaign that ended with Agincourt, Henry V raised 2,000 men-at-arms and 8,000 archers, but by the time of the battle the whole force had been reduced to between 5,500 and 5,900 men. This time the French had some 25,000 men, including about 15,000 men-at-arms.

There were, of course, many non-combatants with any army. There were pages and grooms and light unarmored horsemen called "hobelars," who were a kind of medieval dispatch-rider. There were carters and tradesmen of all sorts – armorers, smiths, "mailers," tent-makers and painters, bowyers and fletchers, carpenters and masons, wheelwrights and cordwainers, saddlers and purveyors of all kinds, quartermasters and farriers. Then there were always several chaplains, a large legal and clerical staff, and musicians – forerunners of the modern band. They were pipers and trumpeters and drummers. As Chaucer says in "The Knight's Tale":

> Pypes, Trompes, Nakirs, Clariouns
> That in the bataille blowen bloudy sounes.

Of course, there were also cooks, bakers, washerwomen, and countless scroungers and hangers-on. So an army of even 10,000 men was not composed of only warriors.

There is no space here to write about the organization of armies, how they were raised, paid, fed, and transported. They could be moved by horse, on foot, by land, and by sea. There is plenty of evidence to show that matters of "logistics" were organized in the Middle Ages in the same way as in the wars of the nineteenth century, right up to the Boer War of

1899-1902 in South Africa. To provide a sense of the reality of medieval war, I want now to look with some detail at four battles that took place between 1191 and 1515; in order to provide the proper context, let's also look at the historical events and situations that led up to those battles.

The Battle of Arsuf, 1191

The siege lasted two long years, pitting the army of the Crusaders against the Saracens, nomadic Muslims engaged in a grueling war. Held down around the city of Acre, the Crusaders refused to relent. After all, Acre was one of the Saracens' most important strongholds – and the Crusaders were a vast army, an enterprise commanded by three of the principal monarchs of the West: Richard I of England, Philip II of France, and Archduke Leopold of Austria, a hot-tempered prince so fond of the bottle that his nickname in some circles was "Sponge." The great crusading army dearly desired the great fortress of Acre, which the Saracens had captured in 1188 under the leadership of Sultan Salah-ed-Din. In July 1191, even the sultan, a great soldier known to his foes and to history as Saladin, had failed to break up and drive off the crusading army of the Franks (as the Saracens always called the people of Europe). So on July 12 the two emirs in command of the garrison decided to surrender – finally.

More romantic tales have emerged from the

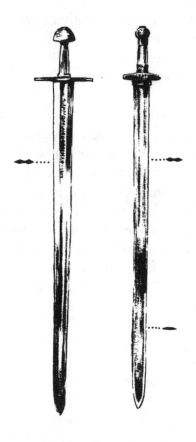

European and Muslim swords. On the left, a typical knightly sword of c. 1150 in the armories of the Tower of London. I have drawn it as it was when in use. On the right, a Muslim sword of the same period, from the collection of the late Professor Storm Rice. At this date, and all through the crusading period (from 1099 until just after 1300), Muslim swords were straight. The curved sword, which was of Eastern European origin, only began to be used by Turks, Arabs, Persians and Indians after the beginning of the 14th century.

Siege of Acre than from any other event in those long and terrible wars known as the Crusades, even though they lasted for nearly 200 years, from 1099 until 1291, when the Christians were finally driven out of Palestine. The Siege of Acre's fame is understandable, for the two most colorful and glamorous leaders of the whole crusading period – Saladin and Richard the Lionhearted – commanded the opposing peoples who fought these wars. On one side were the Arabic nations whose own lands were Palestine, Syria, and Egypt; on the other side were Christians from Western Europe who thought they had every right to steal these lands, to conquer and rule them, because these areas comprised the Holy Land of the Christian faith. The Christians called the Muslim Arabs "infidels" (which means "not of the [true] Faith") or "the foul Paynim" and all sorts of other contemptuous names. The Arabs also spoke of the Christians as "infidels" and gave them other names, such as "Christian dogs," "Giaours," and so on. There was deep hatred between the two opposing religions, though, curiously enough, individual Arab and Frankish people often liked and respected each other a great deal. If it had been left to the soldiers of both sides, the wars would have stopped almost as soon as they began; but unfortunately, it was not. The Christian churchmen and the religious leaders of the Muslims saw to it that the fight was waged relentlessly, gruesomely, bitterly.

In the Third Crusade (as it was called) or The Crusade of the Kings, the Christians were led by three monarchs – from England, France, and Austria. A fourth monarch, the great Frederic Barbarossa (Red-Beard), emperor of Germany, was to have joined them, but he died on his way to the Holy Land. Philip II of France was a small, unwarlike and most unglamorous monarch, and Leopold of Austria was a comical figure. This left Richard of England – Coeur de Lion, as his contemporaries called him – as the outstanding leader of the Christians. He merged charisma with warrior-like qualities: he was a handsome, tall, cheerful man, a tremendous fighter, a most competent and successful man-at-arms, and a born leader. He had a ferocious, terrifying temper as well. His enemies feared him and his friends admired him, and ordinary fighting men, whatever their nation, loved him.

At this time the rule of all the different small Arab or Saracen princedoms had fallen into the hands of a character similar in heroic mien to Richard, yet almost the exact opposite in many other ways. In contrast to the large Richard's golden strength, Salah-ed-Din was dark and small, quiet and grave in manner, and cool in temper where Richard was hot. But Saladin, a great soldier, was as much a hero as Richard. Around these contrasting characters a whole mass of legends, stories, poems, and myths have emerged; some of these tales are pure fiction, but many are true, and even the legends are based upon actual happenings.

Though much has been told and written about the great Siege of Acre, little has been discussed of the intriguing and telling battle that emerged from Acre, a battle that witnessed an important event: Richard's decisive defeat of Saladin.

Each of these great leaders, Richard and Saladin, respected the other and knew the other's worth, but by the time Acre was back in Christian hands, relations between the two had become extremely bitter. Saladin and his enormous army had done everything they could to keep Acre, but to no avail. When it was clear Acre could not be saved, the two emirs in charge of the garrison asked the Christian kings for terms of surrender. The emirs promised they would persuade Saladin to pay a large ransom for the lives of the 2,600 or so men of their army who survived. Richard and Philip agreed, and Acre's gates were opened to the Christian host.

But when it came to dealing with Saladin, a fatal impasse was reached. Richard and Philip couldn't come to terms with the Saracens' leader – they had asked too steep a price for the prisoners. Then Philip, who hated Richard like poison, headed home to France, leaving his army in the charge of the duke of Burgundy and Henri, count of Champagne. Richard was infuriated. He knew that Philip, upon returning to France, would try to stir up trouble with England, which in Richard's absence was being ruled by his nasty and unreliable brother, John. When the negotiations with Saladin broke down, Richard was in a foul mood. His purpose – the stated purpose of the whole Crusade – was to recover the Holy City of Jerusalem and restore the Frankish kingdom in

Palestine. Richard and his army needed to move on; they had no inclinations to hang back in Acre, lumbered with so many infidel prisoners. So on Tuesday, August 20, 1191, he and his War Council made a bloody decision: they ordered the prisoners massacred. After that, any kind of settlement with Saladin was beyond hope. Only one possibility remained: a fight to the death.

Two days later, the crusading army set out for Jerusalem, but it was impossible to march there directly from Acre: the mountains of Ephraim blocked the way, and there was no route for an army to cross them. The best marching route was down the coast to the port of Jaffa. So along the ancient road, trodden 2,000 years earlier by the Pharaohs' armies, the large mixed army of the Franks began its southward march. The road ran only a mile or so inland from the sea, and Richard arranged that the allied Christian fleet should sail parallel along the coast and carry most of the supplies for the army, putting stuff ashore wherever possible. This procedure was not frivolous; it was very necessary, for although the number of fighting men in the army was large for those times – perhaps as many as 8,000 men – they lacked transport wagons and packhorses. While ships carried the bulk of the supplies of food for the men and fodder for the horses, things that were needed daily and constantly, like tents and arrows and crossbowbolts, had to be carried by the infantry. Nearly half of the foot-soldiers had to be used in this way as porters, and so could not be put in the fighting line. No food at all could be gotten on the line of march, for Saladin had adopted a "scorched earth" policy and destroyed or carried off everything that could be of use to the crusaders. He also had dismantled the towns they would have to pass through – Haifa, Caesarea, and Arsuf. The army thus depended entirely upon what it and the supply ships could carry.

Richard had to devise a march-formation that would give his army the optimum chance to form instantly into a line of battle, for there was no doubt the Saracens would use every opportunity to swoop down from the hills on the inland side of the road to harass and, if possible, break the crusading army. So Richard arranged his army this way: He dispensed with the customary vaward, main-battle, and rearward, and divided his fighting men into numerous small units. Next to the sea marched the pack animals and those infantrymen told to carry loads. Inland was the cavalry, in small compact squadrons spaced out at equal intervals along the line of march. Inland again were fighting infantrymen, organized in a solid unbroken column covering the whole eastern flank – the point from which any attacks would come. These infantrymen marched so close to each other that there were no gaps between them. Yet they were organized into twelve units, with one cavalry squadron attached to and marching alongside each unit. There were, then, twelve foot divisions and twelve horse-riding squadrons; but these twelve were, for purposes of organization, joined into five main administrative units whose exact composition is uncertain.

The posts of greatest danger, the leading position (or "van") and the rear-guard, were manned by professional soldier-monks, the Templars and the Hospitallers. They took turns at each post on alternate days during the march. In the center of the army moved the royal standard of England, the staff of which was fixed to a great covered wagon drawn by four horses. Richard and his personal following, the knights of his household, had no fixed position but moved about backward and forward along the line, ensuring that everything was done as it should be.

Armies of this period had three basic types of warrior, some on horse, some on foot: there were men-at-arms, professional infantry, and crossbowmen. First, let's consider men-at-arms – *gens d'armes* as the French called them or *homines ad armas* in Latin. They were the heavy cavalry, fighting with lance and sword, armored in mail from head to foot and riding "barded" and "covered" horses which, for those times, were quite big and heavy – though not in any way to be confused with modern cart-horses. The average courser of a man-at-arms only stood about 14½ to 15 hands. Men-at-arms were of two sorts, knights and sergeants. We know what knights were; sergeants were armed exactly the same, though a wealthy sergeant might have a much better horse and arms than a poor knight. But sergeants did not belong to the high and exclusive society that gave the knight his special, almost mystical, character as a warrior par excellence. In a medieval army, knights were officers; sergeants were ordinary troopers. Next, let's examine the professional infantry, often called foot-sergeants in England. Compared to men-at-arms, foot-sergeants were lightly armed, with their chief weapon being a spear about six feet long. Then came the arbalestiers, or crossbowmen; like the later Swiss, they were professional mercenaries; most of them came from the low countries, then the provinces of Holland, Hainault, Brabant, and so on. Ordinary folk usually called these professional crossbowmen *routiers,* a word that means "highwaymen," for basically that's what most of them were – professional highway robbers turned professional soldiers for pay and pardon. They were the scum warriors of Northern Europe, hated and despised by nearly everyone, but essentially able-bodied, capable, and often brave.

During the Christian army's march to Jerusalem, the August heat hit hard. But Richard would not be foolish. He took great care that his men, suffering from the heat inside their armor, should not be overextended by long marches; so he went slowly, marching only in the early morning and making camp as soon as the day began to get hot. During most of the nineteen days of the march he rested the army completely on every alternate day, once or twice giving them a full 48 hours off. Some of his marches were only of two or three miles, none more than thirteen. This extreme care and thoughtfulness for his troops was one reason Richard was so popular with them.

While marching, the Christian army was harassed by continual swift attacks from the

Saracens, whose fighting methods were quite unlike those of the Christians. Almost every Saracen warrior was a bowman, his bow short and not powerful, his arrows light, but his aim true. The typical Saracen shot from the saddle with great accuracy. The Saracens would attack at high speed, hundreds of yelling men swarming on wiry, fast little horses galloping hard; as the Saracens approached, their arrows flew before them; they never charged home, but kept moving, suddenly wheeling to the side as they got near their opponents. The Saracens moved like a flock of starlings, always together and swarming, and as they did so they continually shot arrows sideways, and then back over their shoulders while retreating. In this way they did little damage to a line of armored Franks that held steady, but if a Christian fighting line broke under the hail of arrows and individual Crusaders charged out upon their gadfly adversaries, they were rapidly surrounded and cut up, while bands of other Saracen horsemen burst into the gaps with sword and spear.

There are many excellent and vivid first-hand accounts of this crusade, as of most of the fighting during the other crusades, thankfully from both the Saracen and the Christian sides. The best accounts are from the writer of the *Itinerarium Regis Ricardi* (The Operations of King Richard) on one side and a Saracen gentleman-soldier named Boha-ed-Din on the other. The *Itinerarium* gives a good description of the Saracens' attacks during these hot days of marching along the coast:

The Infidels, not weighed down with heavy armor like our knights, but always able to out-strip them in pace, were a constant trouble. When charged they are wont to fly, and their horses are more nimble than any others in the world; one may liken them to swallows for swiftness. When they see that you have ceased to pursue them, they no longer fly but return upon you; they are like tiresome flies which you can flap away for a moment, but which come back the instant you have stopped hitting at them: as long as you beat about they keep off: the moment you cease, they are on you again. So the Turk, when you wheel about after driving him off, follows you home without a second's delay, but will fly again if you turn on him. When the king rode at them, they always retreated, but they hung about our rear, and sometimes did us mischief, not unfrequently disabling some of our men.

Saladin's purpose in making these attacks was not only to weary the Christian fighting men, but to break them up, dismantle their organized, effective marching. Most of Saladin's raiding bands were small – often only fifty or even thirty strong – but he had his main army close by, paralleling the line of march at the foot of the hills. His hope was that the Franks, as they had so often and disastrously done in earlier fights, would become infuriated and dash out in chase. If only they would do this, he could come

roaring down with a strong force and burst into the gaps. But Richard knew the danger all too well, and he kept his big mixed army in a state of disciplined control that was rare in medieval war. Nobody charged out; the infantry marched doggedly on, hunched against the arrows, while the armored knights paced slowly along on their right. Here and there a man would fall when an arrow found his eye or an unprotected spot in his body-armor, and many a horse was wounded and some were killed; but steadily the march went on.

Only the king and his meinie – who had no fixed post in the force – allowed themselves the pleasure of dashing out whenever one of the enemy bands got within reach. Many gallant feats of arms were accomplished in this way, though not much damage done; but the panache and glittering splendor of their thundering charges was a wonderful tonic for the foot-slogging infantry.

Boha-ed-Din offers a vivid account of the organized marching and tough demeanor of the Crusaders. Here is how he described some events of August 31:

> The enemy moved in order of battle: their infantry marched between us and their cavalry, keeping as level and firm as a wall. Each foot-soldier had a thick cassock of felt, and under it a mail-shirt so strong that our arrows made no impression on them. They, meanwhile, shot at us with crossbows, which struck down horse and man among the Muslims. I noted among them men who had from one to ten shafts sticking in their backs, yet trudged on at their ordinary pace and did not fall out of their ranks. The infantry were divided into two halves: one marched so as to cover the cavalry, the other moved along the beach and took no part in the fighting, but rested itself. When the first half was wearied, it changed places with the second and got its turn of repose. The cavalry marched between the two halves of the infantry, and only came out when it wished to charge. It was formed in three main corps: in the van was Guy, formerly King of Jerusalem, with all the Syrian Franks who adhered to him; in the second were the English and French; in the rear the sons of the Lady of Tiberias and other

troops. In the center of their army there was visible a wagon carrying a tower as high as one of our minarets, on which was planted the King's banner. The Franks continued to advance in this order, fighting vigorously all the time: the Muslims sent in volleys of arrows from all sides, endeavouring to irritate the knights and to worry them into leaving their rampart of infantry. But it was all in vain: they kept their temper admirably and went on their way without hurrying themselves in the least, while their fleet sailed along the coast parallel with them till they arrived at their camping-place for the night. They never marched a long stage, because they had to spare the foot-soldiery, of whom the half not actively engaged was carrying the baggage and tents, so great was their want of beasts of burden. It was impossible not to admire the patience which these people showed: they bore crushing fatigue, though they had no proper military administration, and were getting no personal advantage. And so they finally pitched their camp on the farther side of the river of Caesarea.

From August 29 to September 6 Saladin had been trying to force an attack. He had to stop the Christians before they got to Jaffa, and he resolved to try a desperate attack at a point between a river-mouth called the Nahr-el-Falaik (Boha-ed-Din's

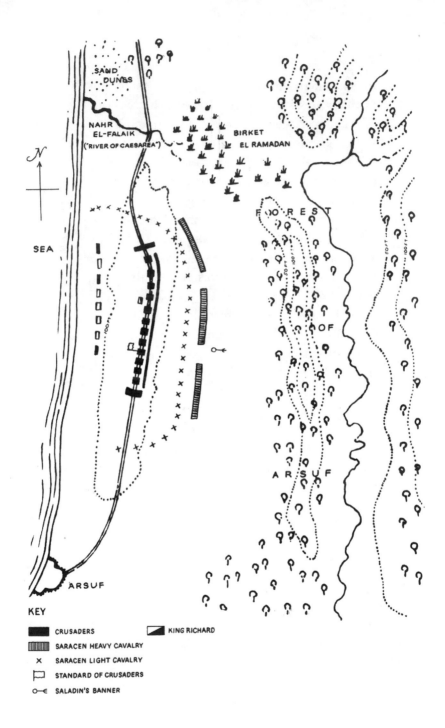

SAND DUNES

NAHR EL-FALAIK
("RIVER OF CAESAREA")

BIRKET EL RAMADAN

N

SEA

FOREST OF ARSUF

100FT
100FT
100FT
100FT

ARSUF

KEY

CRUSADERS

KING RICHARD

SARACEN HEAVY CAVALRY

× SARACEN LIGHT CAVALRY

STANDARD OF CRUSADERS

SALADIN'S BANNER

"River of Caesarea"), and the ruined town of Arsuf. Here he could hide his army, for thick woods covered the foothills to the east of the road for twelve miles, almost as far as Arsuf. A dense oak forest covered all the lower spurs of the hills and reached in some places to within 3,000 yards of the beach. Two days of Richard's march – September 5 and September 7 – would occur between these woods and the sea. Richard guessed what his adversary would do, so on the 5th he issued a special order: his troops must be especially careful not to break ranks, no matter what happened. But the Saracens held back on that day, and on the 6th the Crusaders rested at the Nahr-el-Falaik, their inland flank completely protected by a large marsh, the Birket-el-Ramadan, which lay inland from the river mouth.

Early on the morning of September 7, Richard gave orders to march; the army had to cover the six miles from the river to Arsuf. The road here lay about three-quarters of a mile from the beach, passing along a low ridge. Between the road and the wooded hills was a shallow valley running parallel with the road, varying between one and two miles in width. The Crusaders all knew, as the light strengthened, that Saladin's large army was concealed in the woods; they could see his mounted scouts in all directions.

On this day the Templars took the van position, with their Turcopoles – lightly armored horsemen fighting with bows in the Saracen manner – and foot-sergeants. The next three divisions consisted of

Richard's own Continental subjects, the men from Brittany and Anjou forming the No. 2 division and the men of Poitou, under Guy de Lusignan, the so-called King of Jerusalem, forming No. 3. In the fourth division were the English and Normans with the great banner. The next eight divisions consisted of the French contingents and the men of the Frankish barons of Syria; and guarding the rear came the Hospitallers. Out on the left flank, between the infantry and the woods, rode a scouting group led by Count Henri of Champagne; Richard rode up and down with his household knights and with the duke of Burgundy, the commander of the French forces. The infantry formed their usual unbroken, steady line, crossbowmen on the outside and spearmen on the inside.

Saladin let the whole Christian army get out of camp and well along the road before launching his attack. Though his tactics were to hit along the entire Christian line, he wanted to attack hardest at the rear – with his main strength. He hoped this method would force the Christian rearguard to stop, thus opening a gap as the rest of the army pressed on. If he could make the Hospitallers either stop or charge out at him, he could roll up the whole of the Frankish army. Saladin knew Richard well, but did not know what this tactic might involve. The Saracen leader was preparing a bloody disaster for himself.

The Crusaders were well on their way when the first attack swept out from the woods. First came swarms of skirmishers on horse and foot – black

Sudanese bowmen, the formidable swift-riding Bedouin and the Saracen horse-archers. Behind came deep columns of supporting squadrons of men on horse – Saladin's own heavily mailed Mameluks from Egypt, and the contingents of all the princes and emirs of Syria, Mesopotamia and Egypt. The whole valley between the road and the woods was suddenly filled with this sea of warriors. As one account described it:

> All over the face of the land you could see the well-ordered bands of the Turks, myriads of parti-colored banners, marshalled in troops and squadrons; of mailed men alone there appeared to be more than twenty thousand. With unswerving course, swifter than eagles, they swept down upon our line of march. The air was turned black by the dust that their hoofs cast up. Before the face of each emir went his musicians, making a horrid din with horns, trumpets, drums, cymbals, and all manner of brazen instruments, while the troops behind pressed on with howls and cries of war. For the infidels think that the louder the noise, the bolder grows the spirit of the warrior. So did the cursed Turks beset us before, behind, and on the flank, and they pressed in so close that for two miles around there was not a spot of the bare earth visible; all was covered by the thick array of the enemy.

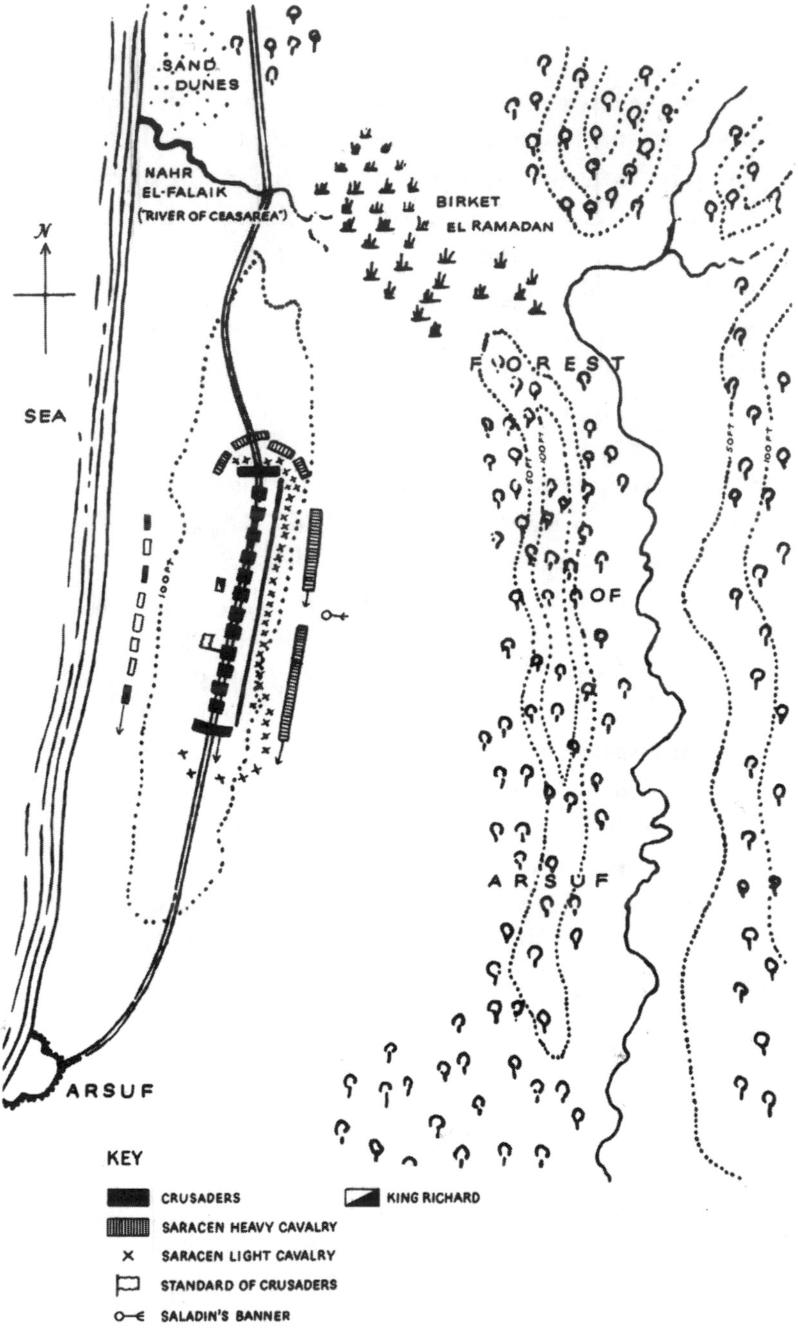
SAND DUNES
NAHR EL-FALAIK ("RIVER OF CEASAREA")
BIRKET EL RAMADAN
N
SEA
FOREST OF ARSUF
ARSUF
KEY
CRUSADERS
KING RICHARD
SARACEN HEAVY CAVALRY
SARACEN LIGHT CAVALRY
STANDARD OF CRUSADERS
SALADIN'S BANNER

Some of the Muslims rode ahead to get between the head of the Christian army and Arsuf, while others followed the rearguard; but most of the Muslims pressed upon the left flank and plied their bows against the plodding wall of Christian infantry and the horsemen slowly pacing behind it. Continual and desperate pressure was upon the Crusaders' rearguard, but the divisions in the front, though harassed constantly, were not seriously annoyed.

Furious as the attack was, for some time the Crusaders forged ahead without wavering. The crossbowmen gave better than they got, for while the light Saracen arrows did them little harm, their heavy bolts, steadily aimed, crashed home through steel and leather with deadly effect. But the Franks' horses did begin to suffer; many knights and sergeants were forced to dismount from fatally wounded horses and take their place with the foot soldiers. Many of the dismounted knights and sergeants picked up crossbows dropped by dead or wounded men and shot down the enemies' horses.

The slow march southward went on, firm and steady, despite everything the Saracens did. Saladin himself charged into the fight, followed only by his two pages leading his spare chargers, urging on his men to press even closer upon the Christian ranks. At the rear of the Crusaders' line things began to go extremely badly, for there the infantry were exposed to arrow-shot from the rear as well as from both sides; some of the crossbowmen faltered, and all were handicapped by having to walk backward with

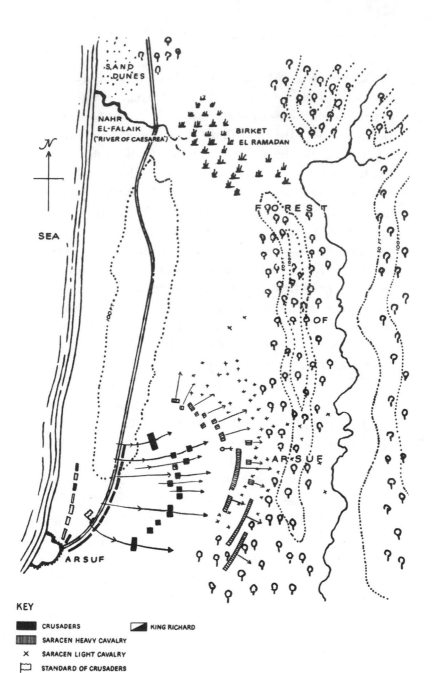

SEA

SAND DUNES

NAHR EL-FALAIK ('RIVER OF CAESAREA')

BIRKET EL RAMADAN

FOREST OF

ARSUF

ARSUF

N

100 FT.
100 FT.
50 FT.
100 FT.

KEY

■ CRUSADERS

▨ KING RICHARD

▥ SARACEN HEAVY CAVALRY

× SARACEN LIGHT CAVALRY

⚑ STANDARD OF CRUSADERS

○—◁ SALADIN'S BANNER

their faces to the pursuing foe, for if they turned their backs for a moment, the Saracens rushed in: "they had left their bows aside now," says the *Itinerarium,* "and were thundering on the rearguard with maces and swords like hammers banging upon anvils."

The Grand Master of the Hospitallers sent galloper after galloper forward to ask King Richard for leave to charge out. The Grand Master was losing all his horses and his knights could not bear the situation much longer, constantly under attack and not allowed to hit back. Richard replied that they must hold fast until hearing his signal – six trumpet blasts – for a general charge. Then they could come out, but not a moment sooner. He wanted to get the whole Saracen host committed to close action all along the line before he rode out. Only the rear of the Crusading army had been seriously engaged; the van and center were being harassed only from a distance. If his knights charged out now, the enemy was far enough off to ride clear and escape. He wanted to annihilate Saladin's army, not just drive it away. Besides, once his van reached the outer houses and gardens of Arsuf, they could take cover and use the town as a defensive position.

The Hospitallers held on, but horse after horse fell and knight after knight was wounded in face and neck and hands and feet, wherever mail provided no protection; the Hospitallers grew restless. At last, just when the van was only a couple hundred yards from the walls of Arsuf, the Hospitallers could bear it no longer. Their marshal and a knight named Baldwin de Carron suddenly wheeled their horses, and, while yelling "St. George! St. George!" the knight and marshal burst through the infantry and rushed upon the enemy. The knights near them followed, then the French knights in the division in front went, and the movement began to spread all along the line.

Richard, seeing what was happening, made the best of it and ordered the trumpets to sound the general charge. Few men that morning realized it was an undisciplined breakout; the Saracens certainly didn't. "Suddenly," says Boha-ed-Din, "we saw the enemy's cavalry, which now were bunched together in three masses, brandish their lances, raise their war-cries and dash out at us. The infantry opened up gaps in their line to let them pass through."

The Saracens did not wait to endure the charge of the dreaded knights of the west. This sudden Crusader change from passive, stolid defense to swift, roaring attack sent the Saracens flying at once. Boha-ed-Din was perfectly honest about it:

> On our side, the rout was complete. I was myself in the center: that corps having fled in confusion, I thought to take refuge with the left wing, which was the nearest to me; but when I reached it, I found it also in full retreat, and making off no less quickly than the center. Then I rode to the right wing, but this had been routed even more thoroughly than the left. I turned accordingly to the spot where the Sultan's bodyguard should have served as a rallying-point for the rest. The banners were still upright and the drum beating, but only seventeen horsemen were round them.

At the northern end of the battle, the Christians' rearguard, where the Saracens were already at hand-strokes, the slaughter was fearful. The rush of knights jammed the Saracens' horse and foot into a solid mass that could neither fight nor run, and the knights were able to take bloody revenge for their long trial of endurance. Before the Muslims could scatter, thousands were cut down. At the other end of the line it was a different story, for the Muslims were not close in and the knights in the leading divisions never caught up with them.

The Crusaders chased the Saracens for about a mile, and then halted at the call of Richard's trumpets and began to re-form — another example of discipline most unusual in any medieval army of European knights. In so many earlier fights, after winning a battle in this way, the Crusaders had pursued wild with excitement until the Saracens were able to swing around and cut them down one by one. But this time only a few knights went on to that fate. The Muslims did, however, rally. Richard then signaled for a second charge, and again the Saracens were sent flying; the knights thundered after them for another mile, almost to the wood's edge, then halted again. And again the scattered enemy rallied and prepared to fight; but a third charge drove them into the woods. This was the end; they dispersed in all directions, and Saladin's great army was no more than a rabble of beaten men making furiously for home.

Richard would not risk his men in the woods. The battle was won, and he took his knights rejoicing back across the littered valley to the town where the infantry was making camp. That night many of the Christians went out, up and down the bloody field, stripping the dead and wounded of arms and valuables. They got a good haul, too, for the Muslims had a way of sewing their money into their clothes or their belts. Like the Christians, the Muslims went into battle with their best jewelry and their finest arms.

That night 32 emirs were counted among the dead, and over 7,000 from other ranks. In the Christian host, only one important knight, a few others, and about 700 men fell.

In this battle King Richard's knights fought in the same way as the knights of Francis I at Marignano 324 years later. They charged with long lances, and when they got in close, they brandished sword, axe, or mace. Their tactics were the same — but their armor differed. At Marignano knights charged against pikemen; at Arsuf, it was against mounted bowmen; in the battle of Lincoln in 1217, we will see knights fighting against knights.

The Battle of Lincoln, 1217

A strange battle it was, fought up and down the steep narrow streets of the city of Lincoln on June 19, 1217. King Richard, of England, was dead, slain by a crossbowbolt in France; so was his nasty but efficient brother John – dead, according to a perhaps apocryphal story, from an illness brought on by stuffing himself with peaches and rough cider. England's king was a small, golden-haired boy of nine, John's eldest son Henry. But the kingdom was under the control of a regent, which was fortunate, for the man King John had nominated to take on that tremendous job was a most competent and talented man, the great knight William Marshal, earl of Pembroke. One of the great heroes of medieval Europe, Marshal was the equal in every way of the Black Prince, or Du Guesclin, or Bayard.

At the start of his adventurous life William Marshal was only the poor, landless younger son of a minor Anglo-Norman baron; but after many years as a successful knight-errant and soldier of fortune, he was high in the favor of his king, Henry II of

England. In 1189, a few years before his death, the king had promised to marry William Marshal to one of the richest heiresses in his realm, the 18-year-old Isabel de Clare, countess of Pembroke. This was a great advancement for William, but Henry died before it could be effected. The new king, Henry's eldest son Richard, was actually in arms against his father at the time of the old king's death, but Richard recognized the loyalty William had always shown to the royal house and made sure the marriage to the heiress took place.

At this time William Marshal was 43 years old. In the twelfth century, when men of the knightly class had every reason to expect to be dead before forty, this was a considerable age; by the time he became earl of Pembroke, ten years after his marriage to Isabel, he was 53, and an old man. But he was only beginning a triumphant career as one of Europe's leading statesmen. He served John as loyally and as well as he had served John's father and elder brother, and when John died William Marshal became regent for little Henry III in 1216; Marshal was 70.

When John died, England was in great peril. For years the land had been ravaged by civil war, one group of barons in savage rebellion against King John and another group supporting him. In 1215 the rebels forced John to seal a solemn declaration of their devise, in which he promised to rule according to their wishes. This was the famous Great Charter, Magna Carta, sealed by a defeated monarch in a grassy meadow at Runnymede on the Thames near Reading on a June day in 1215. Instead of bringing the trouble to an end, the sealing of the Charter only made it worse. Thinking they had the king and his supporters just where they wanted, the barons began to behave as if they controlled the realm. But the king had no intention of sticking to the terms of the Charter. He knew, as well as everyone else, that he had been forced to seal it. Two months later full-scale war broke out again, in which John was, at first, completely successful. He took his opponents by surprise when he went on fighting during autumn, and then ravaged the north in a terrible winter campaign.

The barons then appealed to England's enemies for help. The King of Scots brought an army southward and captured Newcastle, and the barons issued a declaration that John was no longer king, and invited the eldest son of the king of France to take the throne of England. Before spring came in 1216 three French armies had landed on the south coast of England, and in May the French prince came to claim the throne. This was Louis, eldest son of Philip II of France, the monarch who had resigned his joint leadership of the Third Crusade outside Acre in 1191. Philip had become one of Europe's leading rulers, perhaps the most efficient French king during the Middle Ages. Already, in 1216, he was known as Philip Augustus because of his growing power and his qualities of statesmanship. He had beaten John out of great possessions in France some years before, and now was Philip's chance to take over England as well. King John, stripped of most of his power and deserted by many of his supporters, retired to his great castle in Corfe in Dorset with his army of hired mercenaries to await events; and during a terrible summer England was ravaged by foreign armies.

John was beaten, but he refused to give up – refused to take the easy way out and let his kingdom fall into the hands of a foreign power. With his mercenaries he broke out of his stronghold and swept up and down the country, treating England, which had deserted him, as if it were enemy country. He is said to have set fire each morning to the house where he had slept the night before; his trail was marked by burnt-out farms and corpse-littered villages. His men carried off the harvests and livestock, burning or slaughtering what they could not carry with them. His force was never strong enough to fight an official battle, but in the lightning raids he made upon the French and the rebel barons, he showed a savage genius for war that outshone the brilliance of his brother and his father. But fate caught up with him.

In September John made a raid into East Anglia, the heart of his enemies' country. He moved so fast his foes could not catch him; he burned their manors and farms, sacked their towns and castles. Early in October he reached Grimsby, then turned back to Lynn, one of the few towns which still held out for him; it has been King's Lynn ever since. Two days later he started for the north again, but he was in too much of a hurry. Trying to cross the estuary of the Welland before the tide was out far enough, he lost all his baggage in the treacherous sands – all his supplies, his pay chests, his own treasure, and the Crown Jewels of England. It broke his heart. He struggled on as far as Sleaford, exhausted and sick. Here he fell violently ill with dysentery; according to an account by a monk, this illness was brought on because he made a pig of himself with peaches and new cider, but this is probably only another of those tales of historical cock-and-bull that monkish chroniclers were so good at inventing to discredit people they disapproved of. Whatever caused the dysentery, it killed him. He got as far as Newark, and died there on the night of October 18/19, 1216.

Just before he died John sent word to William Marshal: John's little son Henry was in God's keeping, and in William Marshal's. "Beg the Marshal," John said, "to forgive me the wrongs I have done him. He has always served me loyally, and he has never acted against me no matter what I did or said to him." Then John told his captains to fight their way to Worcester in order to bury his body in the Cathedral there, near the shrine of the last of the Anglo-Saxon saints, Wulfstan. John was the first of the Norman and Angevin kings to be buried in England.

You can still see John's likeness in the black marble effigy lying on top of his tomb in Worcester Cathedral. The face is probably a good portrait and fits well with what we know of his bad, but somehow attractive, character. Though superbly bad, he had a sense of humor – you can see that in his face – and was an extremely capable ruler and a great warrior.

He knew he was bad, and asked his friends to do something after his death that may have been meant to conceal how bad he was: he wanted his body entombed wearing the habit of a Franciscan friar, perhaps in the hope that being cloaked in religious garb would score him a point or two on the Day of Judgment.

In 1741, 525 years later, the Society of Antiquaries opened the tomb. They found John's skeleton inside, arrayed exactly like the effigy at Worcester Cathedral, with his long sword by his side and spurs on his heels. But instead of the crown worn by the effigy, the skull was resting in the hood of a monk's habit. The tomb was closed again, and there inside the black stone chest below the effigy John lay as his men put him.

When John died, the rebellious barons and their French allies held all of East Anglia and the southeast, but on the whole the west and southwest still held firm for the Crown – a situation similar to the start of the great English Civil War in 1642, when the east and southeast were for Parliament and the west and southwest for the monarchy. In 1216 the rebels were blocked by a line of strong royal castles – Lincoln, Newark, Nottingham, Northampton, Oxford, Wallingford, Windsor, Devizes, and Corfe. And, in an isolated pocket of resistance, the mighty castle of Dover held out against continual siege.

After John was buried, William Marshal and the loyal barons, with Bishop Gualo, official legate of the pope, and Jocelin, bishop of Bath, had young Henry crowned in the cathedral at Gloucester. Standing alone before the high altar, Henry took a coronation oath dictated to him by the bishop of Bath. Then the legate crowned him with a golden bracelet of his mother's, since all the regalia of England had been lost in the quicksands near Lynn. Historian Matthew Paris of St. Albans, who got the story from eye-witnesses, tells how the tough and war-hardened barons, those who were loyal, were moved to tears as they stood before the handsome little boy who had to take up such a tremendous burden in his war-ravaged realm. Then they all swore the oath of fealty and took the crusaders' cross – not for war against far-off infidels, but for a war against the lawless foreign armies that overran the country.

At the time of John's death, England was in a kind of military stalemate. The situation depended upon the castles; while Dover, Lincoln, and the Midland castles held out for the English king, France's Louis could do little to advance his own cause. He had another handicap as well: It turned out that his English allies, the rebellious barons and their forces, were hopeless as soldiers. He had to rely upon his French knights and sergeants and upon his mercenary infantry; and he did not have very large numbers of either. Early in 1217 Louis made a truce with Hubert de Burgh, castellan of Dover; then a quick campaign in East Anglia regained for Louis the castles John had taken during his last autumn sweep, and Louis turned upon Lincoln. The town surrendered to him at once, but not the castle. The heredi-

Mounted sergeant and foot-sergeant

tary castellan of Lincoln castle was a lady, Dame Nicola de la Haye. She would have nothing to do with Louis' envoys when he went to demand the castle's surrender. He had no option but to lay siege to it. He left two of his captains to maintain the siege, while he went back to London.

Meanwhile the regent, William Marshal, launched his own campaign. He knew Louis was anxious to cross over to France to confer with his father. Marshal's moves seem to have been aimed at cutting Louis off and preventing the trip. Consider, for instance, the capture of Rye on the south coast of Kent by one of the most venturesome and competent of the loyal barons, Philip d'Aubigni. Louis, who was in Winchelsea, was thus trapped between d'Aubigni's forces at Rye and the loyal "outlaws" under the

Flemish knight William de Casingham, who were strong in the thick woodlands of the Kent/Sussex border. But Louis did have resources. He was saved by a fleet from France and a force of his own knights who dashed down from London to help him. These two small bands together recaptured Rye, and Louis sailed for France, leaving orders that his own forces were to go back to London where they would be safe.

When the regent and the main royalist army reached the coast they found Louis gone, so they turned back into Hampshire and recaptured many of the castles there. Then on April 23 Louis landed again at Sandwich, with 140 knights, and three days later he was rejoined by his force from London. To us in the late twentieth century, accustomed to hearing about enormous present-day armies, 140 knights may not seem to be a great reinforcement; but they were. For one thing, this reinforcement amounted to a force of probably 400 or more men, for each knight would have about three men with him, sergeants or varlets as they were sometimes called. If we translate a reinforcement of 140 knights into modern terms, it is the equivalent of 140 tanks with their crews – capable of doing damage in a ground war.

The reinforcement was effective, for the regent went back to Oxford; but his campaign did have at least one valuable result – two of the most important English barons who had supported Louis of France decided to turn their coats and come over to the royalist camp. These were the regent's nephew, William Marshal the younger, and old William Longsword, earl of Salisbury, half-brother to King John and little King Henry's uncle. Not only was Salisbury lord of wide lands in southern England, but he had been nearly the only competent military leader on the rebels' side. The regent had gained more than a good captain, for Salisbury's example brought a hundred barons and knights over to the king during the next few weeks.

Events began moving toward a climax. Late in April a large part of Louis' army, seventy of his own knights under the Count de la Perche and some 520 others – English rebels led by Robert FitzWalter, earl of Winchester – joined the force besieging the castle of Lincoln. At the same time, Louis and the rest of his army again laid siege to Dover castle. He had brought an extremely large stone-throwing engine with him from France and had hoped to batter a way in.

But Louis made a mistake that would prove fatal to his cause in thus dividing his forces. William Marshal was at Northampton when he received news of the concentration of the enemy in Lincoln and of Louis' own presence with half his army far away in front of Dover. Marshal saw the possibilities of the situation – and acted.

On May 13, 1217, gallopers rode out of Northampton to all the bands of royalist knights and sergeants in garrison in the Midland castles, calling on them to muster at Newark; in six days a sizeable host was ready to take the field – 406 knights, 317 crossbowmen, and a considerable number of foot-sergeants. With the host under the command of the regent were Earl Ranulf of Chester, William Longsword of Salisbury, Ferrars Earl of Derby, and the fighting Bishop of Winchester, Peter des Roches. Most of the loyal barons came too, as did the professional captain of mercenaries, Fawkes de Bréauté, who had served John so well and who arrived with the remnants of his company of horse and foot soldiers.

As soon as the regent's force was assembled, it marched northwestward toward Lincoln, spending the night of May 18 in the villages of Torksey and Stow some nine miles from Lincoln. Moving off again in the morning, the army climbed on the high ground along which runs the ancient Roman road – Ermine Street – and went toward the north side of the city walls. By going this way the army would have a chance of getting in touch with the defenders of the Lincoln castle, since it was in the northwestern corner of the city. But that would not happen, or at least it would be delayed, if the rebel besiegers chose to come out and fight in the open country at some distance from the walls.

The regent's host was marshalled in four battles, not the usual three: the vaward led by Ranulf Earl of Chester, the second by the regent, the third by the earl of Salisbury, and the fourth by the warrior-bishop of Winchester, Peter des Roches. The whole force of the crossbowmen under their captain, Fawkes de Bréauté, moved forward a mile in front of the main body of knights and sergeants. The baggage followed a mile behind, escorted by a detachment of infantry.

The engines threw burning barrels of pitch or oil-soaked rags, as well as stones, into besieged castles.

The city of Lincoln lies upon the southwestern corner of a high plateau, rising some 300 feet above the flat Lincolnshire plain and sloping steeply down on its southern face to the river Witham. The city is built on this slope. At the top are the castle, in the northwestern angle of the walls, and the cathedral, some 500 yards to the east. The road passes through the suburb of Newport, north of the city, and enters the walls by the North Gate, an ancient Roman gateway that is still there, though it is called Newport Arch now. You still have to pass under it when you drive into Lincoln from the north. Though the road (now the A15) bends sharply to the left and goes around the back of the cathedral, in the thirteenth century it took a different course: the road went straight down the hill to Wigford Bridge, passing between the castle and the front of the cathedral.

The French besiegers of the castle lay within the city walls, and pressed the siege by battering at the south and east walls of the castle with stone-throwing engines. By May 19 they had shaken a part of the curtain-wall, and hoped to see it fall in the next few days. They had good warning of the royalist army's approach, and two of the rebel leaders, Saher de Quincy and Robert FitzWalter, went out to reconnoiter the advancing columns. They soon returned, reporting that the enemy had only a small force. Their advice: attack in the open before the regent's force got near the walls, thus preventing it from getting in touch with the beleaguered garrison. This tactic made good sense, for the army of the rebels inside Lincoln was considerably stronger than the royalists: The rebels had 611 knights and sergeants, while the royals had just 406; the rebels had 1,000 foot soldiers, while the royals had perhaps 600 or so. But the leader of the French contingent, Count de la Perche, who fancied himself the leader of the entire rebels' army, insisted on surveying the situation himself. He returned firmly convinced that the royalist baggage-train and guard, which he could see in the distance, was in fact a fifth "battle," and that his force was out-numbered. He insisted on staying inside the city and waiting upon events.

He imagined his force would be perfectly safe there. It was nearly impossible in the thirteenth century for a relieving force to storm a town protected by ditch and wall without a long siege. You couldn't just charge in by main force. So the rebels sat tight and went on battering the castle walls while the regent's little army drew closer and closer to the wall of the city.

The only precaution the rebels took was to post strong detachments inside each of the city gates, but this left the rear postern-gate to the castle clear. It could not be guarded, for it was in the wall of the castle itself. If the rebel leaders had put a guard outside, every man would have been shot down from the battlements within five minutes. There simply was no cover; besides, the wall stood at the top of a nearly sheer drop, which you can see from the plan (pg 66). William Marshal could get his men through this gate and into the castle, where friends awaited. But Marshal's men would still be prevented from bursting out of the main front gate and into the large open space between the castle and the cathedral, for the large rebel force battering the castle walls could hold the outside of the main front gate. To try a breakout there would be a hazardous operation.

When the royalists got near the city, they were surprised that the enemy would not come out to meet them, so they halted at a cautious distance. John Marshal, another of the regent's nephews, cantered around the northwest corner of the walls and went into the castle by the postern to see how matters stood. He was warmly welcomed by the high-spirited Dame Nicola, who told him her garrison was doing poorly and could not hold out much longer. He stayed only long enough to hear her news, then galloped back to his uncle – quickly and purposely. When they left the postern, John Marshal and his party were chased by a group of rebel knights. But through hard, capable riding, Marshal's party kept ahead of the pursuit and got back safely to the regent.

William Marshal, hearing John's news, decided to send Bishop Peter into the castle to get a better view of the rebels' forces and thus ascertain how they were disposed. The bishop was renowned for his good military sense; the regent could rely upon his appraisal of the situation, whether to put troops into the castle and then sally out of it, or to attack the city gates. So off went the bishop to make a thorough reconnaissance of the town from the high battlements of the castle keep; he then went down and had a good look at the walls of the castle from the inside, and the walls of the town from the outside. What he found there was of great, peculiar interest.

The outer walls of the castle had been built only some forty years before, and their northwestern corner had taken in some ground of a small residential part of the city, which was now a poor quarter pinched in between the castle and the city wall. Before the castle wall was built, this quarter was important enough to have its own gate – the west gate of Lincoln city. When the castle wall was put up, the gate was no use any more; so it had been blocked. But Bishop Peter saw that it was only loosely blocked with dry, unmortared stones. The rebels hadn't troubled to watch this disused gate, partly because, since it was right under the castle wall, there was nowhere for a cat to take cover, let alone a detachment of enemy men.

The good bishop got outside the castle wall by a small concealed door in the wall adjoining this blocked gate and had a careful, close, undisturbed look at it. He was delighted to see that the masonry was so loose and badly set that half-an-hour's determined work could clear it. He nipped back into the castle and suggested to Dame Nicola that she should send men out to clear the gate as soon as the fighting began and the enemy's attention was engaged elsewhere. Then he rode back to the regent, told him what he had found, and made this suggestion: A force should be sent into the castle and make a sortie from its gate, thus distracting the enemy. Meanwhile, the regent's main army should go to the west gate, which would soon be unblocked. He could get straight into the city that way.

The regent sent Fawkes de Breaute with his household knights and all the crossbowmen into the castle; at once the crossbowmen ran to the walls and began to shoot fast and hard at the party of the enemy besieging the castle gate. Many of the enemy's horses were killed, and the whole rebel lot was thrown into confusion as it tried to take cover under the walls. Then Fawkes sallied out with his knights and foot-sergeants and made a vigorous attack on the besiegers, but they were too many for him. His men were beaten back, and he himself was captured for a few moments until some of his knights rushed back to rescue him.

Meanwhile, Earl Ranulf took it upon himself to begin a fierce assault upon the city's north gate. The regent, a gallant old warrior, was getting impatient. For Fawkes was fighting like a tiger inside the castle,

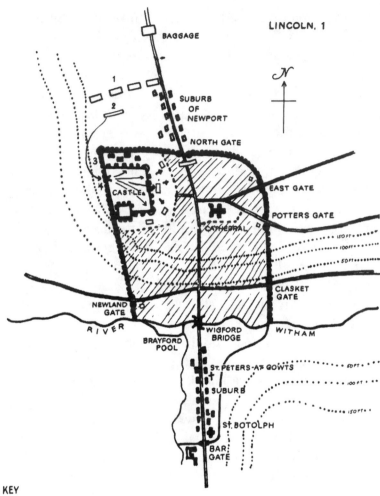

LINCOLN, 1

BAGGAGE

SUBURB
OF
NEWPORT

NORTH GATE

1

2

3

CASTLE

4

EAST GATE

POTTERS GATE

CATHEDRAL

150 FT
100 FT
50 FT

CLASKET
GATE

NEWLAND
GATE

RIVER

BRAYFORD
POOL

WIGFORD
BRIDGE

WITHAM

ST. PETERS-AT-GOWTS

50 FT

SUBURB

100 FT

ST. BOTOLPH

150 FT

BAR
GATE

KEY

1 EARL MARSHAL'S ARMY

2 FAWKES DE BRÉAUTÉ'S FORCE

3 BLOCKED WEST GATE

→ REBELS' "PERRIERS"

///// BUILT-UP AREAS FULL OF
///// HOUSES AND NARROW LANES

4 POSTERN IN CASTLE WALL

and Ranulf and his men were bashing away at the city gate; but the regent, where was he? Sitting on his horse outside the city walls and doing virtually nothing. It was too much for the warrior to bear. "By the lance of God," the regent exclaimed, "give me my helm!" But the cautious Bishop Peter restrained him, persuading him to go forward with ten knights just to see if the blocked gate had been cleared. It had. As Marshal approached it, he could see some of Fawkes' foot-sergeants, repulsed outside the main gate of the castle, come rushing through, closely pursued by some of the enemy. The old knight had enough. "Come on," he yelled, "you can't hold back now. Charge!" But again the bishop stopped him, insisting he should wait for the rest of his men. To charge in with only ten knights was ludicrous. But William wouldn't listen. He put spurs to his horse, but then heard a frantic yell behind him. So he reined in again, savage with impatience. "My lord! – wait, for Mary's sake! Your helm!"

It took a few moments for the regent to quiet his horse enough for his squire to put the great helm on

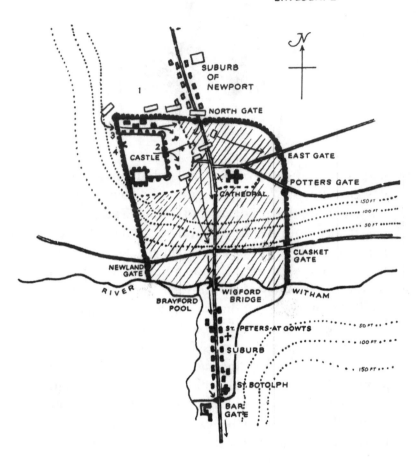

his head and tie the laces at the back of his neck; by the time the regent was properly armed, the rest of his men had come up; nothing could hold him back now, and so he dashed through the west gate with the bishop riding at his side bellowing *"Sa! Dieu aide au Maréchal."*

The royalist army, once it had gotten close to the city among the houses and gardens of the suburb of Newport, seems to have been hidden from the rebels' sight, for nobody interfered with the unblocking of the west gate; and nobody noticed that at one or two points between this disused gate and the north gate, parties of royalist soldiers were actually getting over the wall. The north gate was soon cleared when the rebels holding it were attacked from the flank and rear. Then a royalist party headed by John Marshal got into the open space before the castle and attacked the rebels who were busy repelling de Bréauté's sally. John Marshal's party came in on the side of the besiegers' engines and managed to kill the chief engineer just as he was loading a rock into one of his perriers to shoot at de Bréauté's men. Royalists began pouring into the city, forcing the rebels back into the steep narrow streets leading down to the bridge, and a fierce series of jousts began in all the northwestern streets of Lincoln. Street-fighting on horseback is most difficult, and it was only by applying strong and consistent pressure that the royalists were able to push the rebel horsemen back. The foot-soldiers slipped in among the rebels, killing their horses. In time royalists occupied that part of the city around the castle and the rebels began to fall back, some into the open space in front of the cathedral and some down the main street toward the bridge. The Count de la Perche rallied his French knights and some of the rebels in front of the cathedral, and for a time they held their ground against the regent and his "battle," but at last the count's men broke and scattered. He was surrounded and his surrender was demanded; but he yelled through his helm that he'd never surrender to any lousy Englishman. Then William Marshal kneed the count's horse and grabbed the count's bridle, while a knight named Reginald de Croc — one of de Bréauté's household — cleanly thrust a lance-point through the eye-slit of the count's helm. The count was finished, but before falling off his horse he delivered three tremendous blows upon William's helm, leaving permanent dents.

The French had little heart left for fighting, not with their leader dead and their allies running away. They struggled down the hill into the lower town, where they did rally and attempt feebly to regain their ground; but it was no use, so they made way to the south gate of the city, looking for an escape. But they found none there. The gateway was narrow, and the two leaves of the gate worked with counterweights so that each leaf shut automatically after it had been pushed open, meaning only one person could go at a time unless the gate were fastened back. Imagine a struggling, bawling press of men and horses, all stuck fast, immersed in a confusion made worse when a frantic cow somehow got mixed up in the rout. Here the royalists were able to take prisoner nearly every one in the rebel army who had taken part in the battle, including the three leaders left after de la Perche's death – Saher de Quincy and the earls of Hereford and of Lincoln, as well as several of the rebel barons who had signed the Great Charter two years before.

Not many were killed, though many were wounded. The only knights named as dead were Reginald de Croc on the royalists' side and the Count de la Perche on the rebels' side. Of course, this accounting doesn't consider the lightly armored foot soldiers, of which a good number perished, as well as quite a few of the citizens of Lincoln who couldn't help getting mixed up in the street-fighting; many fleeing mercenary foot-soldiers were butchered, as well, by the local peasantry. No hired foreign soldier's life was worth a brass farthing in the English countryside unless he was in a strong party. Men in twos and threes, especially men on the run, didn't stand a chance.

The plunder or spoils that came to the regent's army in Lincoln was enormous; there was so much that from that evening they began to call the battle "Lincoln Fair," which has been its name ever since.

That battle decided the war, too, though perhaps not as quickly as the military men would have liked. As soon as he heard of his army's defeat, Louis raised the siege of Dover and retreated to London. The victorious regent marched southward, halting at

Chertsey, only 16 miles from London, to meet the
envoys Louis sent out to negotiate for peace. But the
negotiations came to nothing. Though the military
men agreed upon reasonable terms at once, the
churchmen would have none of them. They insisted
upon terms no sensible or honorable baron of
England could agree to, so the war went on. But
things were bad for Louis. More and more of the
English barons returned to their allegiance; his only

hope lay in reinforcements that his father, King Philip II, had promised to send from France.

The threat of these reinforcements worried the regent, and when he heard they had arrived at Calais he was anxious, especially since he didn't know how many – he thought it was 300 knights and their men. By an enormous effort of organization and diplomacy he mustered a fleet – as well as his army at Sandwich. To get a fleet together was no easy business, for the seamen of the Cinque Ports, the backbone of medieval England's naval strength, had been badly treated by King John. But in the face of the threat of yet another foreign invasion, the seamen rallied to the royalist cause. The great sea-battle that followed off Dover on August 25 was a decisive victory. All but fifteen of the French ships were sunk or captured, and 32 Frenchmen of high rank were taken prisoner; the less prestigious survivors were pitilessly slaughtered.

The steep streets of Lincoln are still very much as they were in 1217, and the open space in the upper town between the castle and the cathedral is still there, although there are more buildings on it, including the gateway to the cathedral precincts. But the west front of the cathedral is the same, and the sculptured figures on it, which we can still see, looked down on that violent scene in 1217 as they look down on the area now. It takes little imagination to re-create the whole affair. In the museum at the bottom of the hill you can see a number of fine medieval swords, one of which is probably a relic of

King Stephen's battle of 1141, but some of the others were probably lost in the river by the town's foot on that May afternoon.

Not very much firsthand information remains of those who took part in "Lincoln Fair." But, like the great Bayard, William Marshal did have a "loyal Serviteur" to write his biography. It was done by a knight of his household named John d'Erley, who wrote in verse. Even so, it is remarkable how much alike are his *Histoire de Guillaume le Marechal* and *La Très Joyeuse Plaisante Récréative Histoire* of Bayard, written by a loyal servant who never gave his name to his book, but who was probably Jacques Joffre de Millieu.

William Marshal died in 1219; he was buried, as he had requested, in the church of the Knights Templars in London; and there in the church is a battered effigy in Purbeck marble that was placed above his tomb circa 1250. Even before the blazing roof of the ancient round church fell on it in 1940, most of the features left visible by the mail coif had been worn away; but it was probably never much of a portrait – certainly not like the well-preserved face of King John in Worcester. But it does mark the place where the bones of the great old warrior rest. Similarly, in Salisbury Cathedral is the well-preserved effigy of William Longespée (Longsword), earl of Salisbury, whose body was put into the tomb-chest under the effigy in 1222. In this case the sculptured figure is splendidly preserved, even much of the original color surviving; but the old warrior is shown with his mail coif drawn up and laced tight across his mouth and nose, so we can only guess at his appearance. But if we consider his figure, armed from head to toe, we get a good idea of how he and his companions looked on the morning of "Lincoln Fair."

The Battle of Mauron, 1352

The next battle I want to consider took place during a time of great changes in armaments and tactics. It was fought near the little town of Mauron in Brittany in 1352, during the first part of the Hundred Years' War and 135 years after the regent's great plunder at Lincoln Fair. To understand the changes that make the Battle of Mauron so intriguing, consider the use of weapons in the preceding years. In 1217, for example, a European knight was armed in almost the same way as his Gothic predecessors had been during the final years of the Roman Empire. His battle tactics were nearly the same, too, and it didn't matter whether he was English, French, German, Italian, Spanish or from the Scandinavian countries. It's true that during the thirteenth century wealthy knights began adding extra pieces to their armor, but there was little real, substantive change until about 1325. Then, between about 1325 and 1380, a relatively short span of time, the armor of a well-equipped knight developed into something new: thanks to changes in weaponry, age-old armor of mail no longer served as adequate defense; it was replaced by a complete covering of polished steel plates.

The appearance in Europe of two new weapons led to this change in armor. Before that, mail made for a fine defense, providing a measure of safety against the blows of weapons from the time it was first devised by the Celts in Central Europe around 400 B.C. There had been no need for change – that is, until something dramatic took place. When England's great warrior king, Edward I, seized upon the idea of using the Welsh longbow in the hands of trained English archers as a mass weapon, the days of mail were numbered. Edward I was the son and successor of Henry III (whom we saw in the previous chapter as a boy of nine) and grandson of John, who had spent so much time fighting his barons. Edward carried on an idea that John, because of his battle with rebellious barons, was too busy to put into effect – the idea of unifying the three realms of England, Wales, and Scotland into one kingdom. It was during campaigns in Wales from 1277 until 1289 that Edward saw the possibilities of the Welsh longbow. When he began his campaign to incorporate Scotland into his kingdom, he used large forces of English as well as Welsh bowmen with great effect. His successor, Edward II, no soldier at all, lost all that Edward I had gained in Scotland. The reason? Partly because Edward II had no interest in warfare and partly because he was opposed by that great Scottish hero, Robert the Bruce, King Robert I of Scots, who beat the English out of his land in a series

Sword of c. 1350. This type of sword, with a blade of a stiff section and a very sharp point, came into fashion at the same time as the new plate armor. The old style of flat, springy sword-blade, useful only for cutting, would have been useless against plate armor. (Armories of the Tower of London.)

of stunning campaigns from 1307 to 1314, ending with a great victory at Bannockburn.

Edward II was deposed and murdered by his barons. His young son, Edward III, had one fixed idea: to beat the Scots and avenge his father's disasters. Edward III came to the throne in 1327, when he was only fifteen, and five years later his captains secured a considerable success over the Scots in a ferocious little battle at Dupplin Moor near Dunfermline in 1332. The English were successful because they returned to Edward I's use of the longbow. A second battle a year later at Halidon Hill near Berwick confirmed the awful power of this new weapon. The armor in use at that time was not effective against it. But leading military thinkers in the rest of Europe likely did not take notice of these battles. Even if they heard of the Scots' defeats, they were not aware of the weapon that caused them.

In another corner of Europe, another new weapon was in use for the first time – a great axe, with a spear-point in its head, mounted on a haft between five and seven feet long, and wielded by the ancestors of the Swiss. The tremendous blows of these weapons sheared through reinforced mail defenses as a knife goes through butter. Actually, this sort of weapon had made its debut on a battlefield in Flanders, outside the town of Courtrai, in 1302, where a large army of peasants and townsmen had absolutely smashed to pieces a great force of French knights and men-at-arms splendidly equipped in the very latest fashion. But it was the Swiss who developed this deadly thing (which came to be called a halberd) as their national weapon, a century and a half before they changed to the even deadlier pike. It was their earlier use of the halberd, and the English use of the longbow, that made it plain to the armorers of Italy and Germany that something far better than mail would be needed for defensive armor.

In 1337 a long series of wars pitting England against France came about, known to history as the Hundred Years' War. It was initiated because Edward III was obsessed with his mighty grandfather's dream of uniting England and Scotland. Edward III realized his dream would not come to fruition as long as the French helped the Scots. If he wanted to incorporate Scotland under the English crown, he would have to fight the French first. He was encouraged by the people of Flanders, who had a great interest in England because their principal business was making cloth – they exported it all over the world – and they needed England's wool. But they were vassals of the French monarchy, which they found irksome. It was to their advantage to have England as an ally, not only to supply the wool they needed but to get the French off their necks.

Edward III had a stake in the land of France as well, for the English monarch possessed the territories of Gascony (made up of the provinces of Aquitaine and Guyenne), which had been part of the enormous possessions Henry II had acquired through his marriage with Eleanor of Aquitaine in 1152. Gascony was nominally part of France – the English king had to pay homage to the French king for it – but in fact it was an English possession. So in addition to obtaining a foothold, or bridgehead, through an alliance with the Flemish people in Flanders, Edward III had his own lands in the south. He got a third bridgehead in Brittany, at that time an almost independent duchy that, when the war began in 1337, was in a state of civil war owing to a dispute between the great families of De Blois and De Montfort for the title and power of the duke of Brittany. Edward sided with De Montfort, vigorously supporting their claim, thus giving him good reason to send troops to Brittany; France, opposing Edward, of course supported De Blois; and for decades Brittany became a battleground where countless fights took place between French and English.

The effect of the longbow arrows used by hundreds of first-class marksmen all shooting together, five shots a minute, was first really noticed at the naval battle fought at Sluys in 1340. But initially nothing much was done – at least not effectively – to stop this offensive onslaught. In many fights in

Even swords couldn't cut plate-armor, nor could the sharply pointed, very stiff blades pierce it, so cracking and crushing weapons became popular with knights. These two weapons (from a Spanish painting of c. 1380) have shafts about 3 feet 6 inches long; the axe (above) has a sharp pick at the back, and a long spike in front. The hammer (it was called a maul in 14th-century England) also has a sharp point on the back of the flat hammer-head.

Brittany and Gascony in the years that followed, the archers brought victory to English armies, but it was not until the first major battle of the war, fought at Crécy, that the longbow really made an impression on the military mind of the Continental countries.

The impact of Crécy was stunning. We can see, looking back more than six hundred and fifty years later, how the fashion of a knight's armor seemed to change almost overnight after that August evening in 1346. By 1350, a complete, smooth, close-fitting armor of plate had been devised (probably by the designers in the great arms works in Milan). This armor was about 75 percent effective in keeping the dreadful arrows from penetrating. Looking back from our own time and studying the development of armor, we can see how every manuscript picture, every statue, every tomb-effigy of an armored knight showed one sort of armor – the old reinforced mail – for the 1340s, but a new sort, the complete plate, for the 1350s.

The arrow-flight produced new tactics, too. From Dupplin Moor on, the English used archers in combination with dismounted men-at-arms: an English force would, whenever possible, take up a battle-position where its flanks were protected by woods or steep slopes or marshy ground, through which cavalry could not get at them; the English force would dismount all the knights and sergeants, sending the horses to the rear to be guarded with the baggage-wagons. Then the men-at-arms would be drawn up in a solid block – or several blocks if there were enough of them. The archers would be at each end of the line, or in between the blocks, and at an angle to the line of battle, and from such a position the English force waited for the attack (see the diagram on page 90).

When the attack came, the archers would wait until they couldn't miss – "till they could see the whites of their eyes" – and then let fly. If the enemy attack was mounted, as at Crécy, the horses were shot down so that few men ever got to engage in handstrokes with the English knights. Until Crécy, the French always charged in on horseback, regardless of their inevitable failure to strike home; to a French knight it was absolutely unthinkable to fight on foot. After all, what was a knight for, except to fight splendidly on his horse? But after the terrible,

utter French disaster of Crécy, they saw the hope-
lessness of this chivalric attitude, and from then on
fought mostly on foot. This change didn't help much,
though, for the English always forced them to attack.
While the armored Frenchmen slogged up slopes or
across muddy fields, arriving at their foe's battle line
out of breath and too tired to fight properly, the
English sat in comfort and waited for them to arrive,
beaten before they struck a blow.

Just how was such a battle fought? What were
the immediate effects of a particular battle fought in
this way? Just how devastating could such a battle be
– and how triumphant? Let's see.

On a fine sunny morning in August 1352 an
English knight rode out of the town of Mauron onto
the bare hilltop outside its walls. He was Sir William
Bentley, in command of a small striking-force of
English and Breton men-at-arms, some 1,200 of
them, and about 1,800 English archers. His object
was to meet, and if possible defeat, a big French army
marching across Brittany and intent upon capturing
the port of Brest. Earlier in the day, while his force
rested in town, he had heard that the French army
had turned off the direct road to Brest and was moving southward to Mauron with the singular purpose
of bringing on a battle. The French force under the
marshal Guy de Nesle was much larger than
Bentley's English and Breton army, and seemed likely to defeat it easily.

Sir William needed to find a good defensive

position from which to draw up his men in what has now become the traditional English manner. The town behind him stood on a low hill with a bare grassy spur jutting out to the east, sloping down to a little stream about 1,200 yards from the walls. A belt of trees was between the town wall and the stream; otherwise, the hill and slopes down to the valley were bare. Sir William looked around the smiling summer landscape, large unhedged fields rolling away to the horizon. Down the slope on his right was a small château called Brembili with its orchard and gardens. The slope was gentle there, but in front of him to the left it was much steeper, dropping sharply down some 100 feet to the stream and then rising abruptly on the far side. A road into Mauron ran parallel with the stream for a short way through the steep dip – the road from Rennes, along which the French were coming. Sir William shaded his eyes with his hand, looked to the northeast, and saw a haze of dust in the distance. Yes, they were coming all right. He wheeled his horse and galloped back to town.

In a few minutes Sir William's army began to emerge from the east gate of Mauron onto the top of the spur. With his second-in-command, Sir Robert Knollys, he rode up and down while putting his men into position. It was an awkward field, for his army was too small to stretch from side to side of the slightly narrower neck of the spur, and there were no woods upon which he could secure his flanks. If he drew them up in line with one end resting on the gardens of the chateau and the other on the edge of the sharp dip on the left, his center would be much higher up the slope of the rounded hill than his flanks. Still, it would have to do. He divided his archers into two bands of some 600 each; one band he stationed on his right flank against a trackway that ran between Mauron and the village of St. Levy, with the garden wall of Brembili on the other side; and the other he placed above the dip on the left flank. His men-at-arms were drawn up, on foot, across the top of the slopes.

The French had no immediate obstacle to hinder them, for the stream was small enough to step over; but the slope in front of the English position was covered with long rank grass and dotted with gorse bushes. If the French advanced on foot, as they had taken to doing, this growth would eventually slow them down a good deal.

Sir William and Sir Robert rode along their line, seeing how dangerously thin it was. The front extended for some 700 yards, a long position to be held by less than 3,000 men. There was no chance to form a second line or a reserve. Every man had to go into the front rank. Sir William and Sir Robert rode back to the top of the hill to see how the enemy was progressing.

Soon the French army's leading columns appeared on the road from Rennes; it became painfully obvious to the two English knights that the French greatly outnumbered them. It was obvious to the French commander, too, for he could see how thin the enemy line was as it formed on the hill above him. The French commander waited until his army had come up and spread into the fields facing the hill; he then courteously sent a herald to Sir William to inform him that, if he promised to leave Brittany, he could take his army off unattacked and unharmed. Sir William's reply was a scornful refusal.

It was now almost two-thirty in the afternoon; the English and the Bretons sat or lay on the grass while the herald came and went, and the French army began to form in battle array in the fields below. In the drowsy afternoon heat the hum of insects in the lush grass mingled with the rumble of voices, the stamping of feet and hooves, and the rattle of harness and armor as the French got into posi-

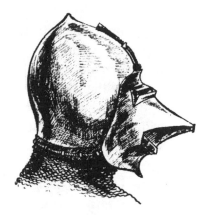

The visor of this kind of "bascinet" was fastened on by a single turning-pin fitting on the forehead of the helmet, which engaged in a slot in a hinged staple at the top of the visor. The German name of Klappvisier ("snap-visor," because you snap it on) is used for this type. Examples surviving are rare, but there is one in the armories of the Tower of London.

tion. Every now and then the level of sound was pierced by a shouted order, a trumpet's blare, or a primitive insult hurled between army and army.

Sir William, still at his post on the highest point of the slope, watched the French forming. There was a good deal of movement down there; the horses had been watered at the stream and led back up the gently sloping field behind, but now some of them were having bits put back into their mouths. Were the French going to ride after all? He held his breath, then let it out slowly. No, only some of them. That was to be expected – probably two squadrons to ride in on the flanks. He continued watching as the French men-at-arms mounted. No, it would be only one lot, on the left, and it was evidently going to charge across the field against the archers on his right.

Slowly the great mass of French men-at-arms formed up, a long, solid wall of armored men facing the English line; at about four o'clock the harsh trumpets pealed and the French nakers – a sort of kettle drum – began to beat a steady, rattling rhythm. The long line lurched forward and began to cross the stream.

On the hill, the English and Bretons got to their feet. The archers tightened their belts, checked bowstrings and the bracers on their left arms, put on their iron hats, and strung their great bows. The men-at-arms tightened straps they had previously loosened while they rested: men who preferred to cover their faces with visors fixed the visors to their bascinets before putting them on, and every man settled himself into the hot embrace of his armor and lowered his lance to present a hedge of steel points to the advancing foe.

Slowly the French approached, all along the line. On the English left, the archers began to shoot "wholly together," and though many arrows glanced harmlessly off the plated enemy, many of the French fell. On the English right, where the French cavalry charged up a very easy slope, it was different. The English archers got off six or seven volleys, and many horses of the French fell or threw their riders, but it wasn't enough confusion to stop the charge. The French army crashed home upon the archers, who stood at handstrokes for a few moments before beginning to move back up the hill. This movement exposed the flank of the line of English men-at-arms, who had to start moving back as well. Soon the right wing of the English line was bending dangerously.

On the left, the English situation was better, for the archers stood fast. As the French, hunched against a shower of arrows, trudged in ever more slower steps up the tangly slope, their numbers thinned more and more. At last, before they had even reached the English line, the French men-at-arms turned and began to run and stumble down again. With a roar of triumph, the English archers – most of their arrows already shot – drew their swords and plunged down after the retreating French. Many a rich ransom was won by humble archers that day, and for many a non-noble French sergeant the last

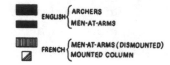

KEY TO BATTLE OF MAURON PLANS:

ENGLISH { ARCHERS / MEN-AT-ARMS

FRENCH { MEN-AT-ARMS (DISMOUNTED) / MOUNTED COLUMN

MAURON. DIAG. 1

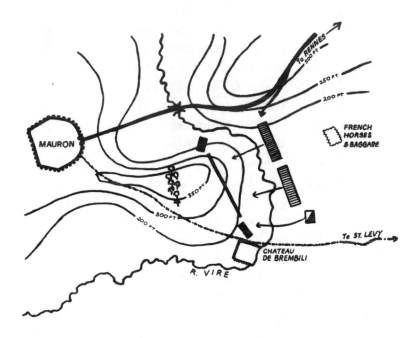

thing he saw was the glitter of a dagger through the eye-slit of his visor.

In the center, the push was tremendous. Even though the French right had fled, the English were still greatly outnumbered. They gave a few paces — held, hacking and thrusting, then gave a few paces

KEY TO BATTLE OF MAURON PLANS:

ENGLISH { ARCHERS / MEN-AT-ARMS

FRENCH { MEN-AT-ARMS (DISMOUNTED) / MOUNTED COLUMN

MAURON. DIAG. 2

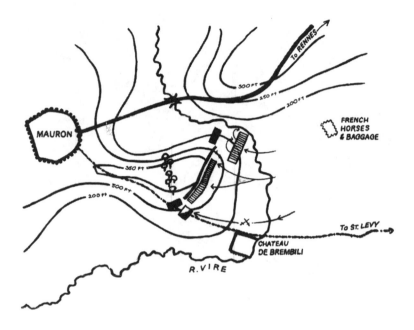

more. The archers on the English right, some running away, went back to the line of trees. The English
line was bent, and the knights fought now with their
backs to the trees. Then, suddenly, the pressure on
the English eased. In the howling, clashing confusion
of wailing voices and hammering blows, new notes

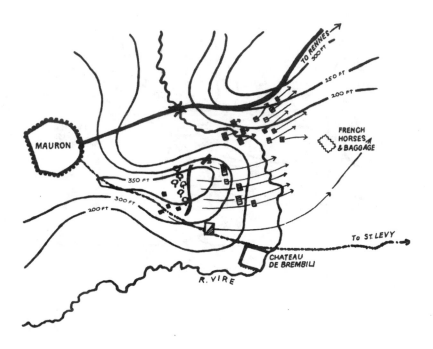

could be heard: shouted orders, cries for help, the easing of even more pressure, and the continued advancement of the English. After a few minutes, instead of peering at the monstrous blank steel faces of the Frenchmen's visors, the English were looking at their enemy's backs.

The archers' success on the left of the line had saved the day for the English. When the French men-at-arms began to give way in that part of the battle, they left their comrades' flank open. The archers, and the men-at-arms on the English left (who had yet to strike a blow), turned inwards and began to roll the French line up.

After that, victory was swift and complete for the English. Plate armor might keep some arrows out, but it was not meant for walking in, thus making fighting and retreating most difficult. The French paid the consequences. Tangled in the long grass, their legs caught by the scrubby gorse bushes, the French, exhausted by their climb up the slope, couldn't get away. Those who were lucky enough to get off from the rear ranks did manage to cross the stream. But, as they lumbered toward their horse-lines, they were caught on the far side by nimble, unarmored English archers.

The English and Bretons in the center had been so busy that they at first did not realize their leader, fighting like a tiger, suddenly sank to the ground under their trampling feet. Luckily somebody must have seen him fall and dragged him back to the trees, for when the fighting stopped they found him there seriously wounded. They counted their prisoners: they had 160 knights and esquires. Then they went into the field and counted the dead. They came upon the battered body of Guy de Nesle, marshal of France, and some of his knights. The English and Bretons also came upon the bodies of 140 others, including numerous sergeants. The total loss to the French army was some 2,000 dead and not quite 200 prisoners. The rest had fled. The greatest French loss had been to the men-at-arms on foot; the mounted squadron got away with few casualties.

On the English side there were few deaths; the most serious were 30 archers of the broken right wing, who were hanged the day after the battle by Sir William because they ran away. That was harsh treatment, indeed, but perhaps the urgency of the situation and his own painful wounds caused Sir William to be especially merciless.

The decisive result of this battle settled the war in Brittany for many years to come. Sir William Bentley's force won not just because of the English archers, nor just because the English and their Breton allies could fight better than the French and their Breton allies. Bentley won with morale, that strange psychological factor that enters into warfare and often produces curious effects. After Crécy, the French had come to fear the English and to dread their archers in particular – and with good reason. As for the English, well, they had often had great confidence in themselves as fighters, but by 1352 their fighting psyche became even more implacable and insolent: they were absolutely convinced that they could knock hell out of the French, however heavy the odds might be, and that one English knight could take on any number of French and overcome four with only one hand. Such thinking may be jingoistic, yes, but it can make a fighting force unified and strong. For when every man in an army believes in the power that is in his blood and is part of his birthright, that army can be extremely hard to beat. Many extraordinary examples of this spirit emerged in the next ten years in France. The great September 1356 victory at Poitiers by the Black Prince of Wales is one example, but some of the small, almost unrecorded, skirmishes show this morale factor even more vividly.

In the spring of 1356, Henry, duke of Lancaster (Edward III's cousin and one of the great captains of the age), took a small force, a bit like Sir William Bentley's four years earlier, on a great raid through Normandy. There isn't space to study it in detail here, but it was entirely and astonishingly successful. Henry's force captured many castles, brought back a host of prisoners, 2,000 horses taken from the French, and an enormous lot of valuable loot. But the high spots of the raid were two skirmishes that took place just as Lancaster's force was getting back toward its base at La Hogue on the coast; the French, hoping to cut the English off from this base, broke down a bridge across the river Vire at a village called St. Frommond and left 60 men-at-arms and some other soldiers waiting in ambush, ready to cut up Lancaster's advance guard. Fifteen English men-at-arms were all that rode ahead of the force, and they ran into the ambush; but the English killed all the Frenchmen without losing one of their own.

Next day the army reached Carentan, more or less home; and on the morrow they got to

Montebourg. In charge of the base camp near La Hogue was Sir Robert Knollys; when he heard the army was so near, he rode out with seven men-at-arms to meet them; they too ran into a French ambush of 120 men. As one account put it: "And the said Robert and seven men-at-arms slew them all except three, which were taken to ransom!" The French were soon to call Sir Robert Knollys "Robert le Terrible," for as one of Edward III's captains of Free Companies he made a name for himself up and down France in the next twenty years. When it came to fighting, he was terrible indeed.

The Battle of Marignano, 1515

In the closing years of the fifteenth century, France's situation had changed from what we saw at Mauron. The Hundred Years' War with England had been over since 1453, and all England's hopes of Continental dominance had been shattered: the English, except for the garrison of Calais, had been thrown out of France, while England itself had been brought to near ruin by the so-called "War of the Roses," the long civil war between rival groups of barons who sought to control the rival kings, Henry VI of Lancaster and Edward IV of York. France, nearly destroyed by the long wars, had slowly and painfully lifted itself up, from about 1429 onward, and had begun to turn the tables. The French began to beat the English as once the English had beaten them. The reason, as we saw after Mauron, was a case of morale, the morale of a nation inspired by a hero – though in France it was a heroine: Jeanne d'Arc, the Maid of Orléans.

Once the English had been cleared out, France soon recovered. This recovery was greatly helped by the king it crowned in 1461, Louis XI. He was an efficient and businesslike monarch, and in his reign between 1461 and 1483 he built France again into a great nation, so much so that in 1493 his son, Charles VIII, was able to contemplate the possibility of setting off with a great army to conquer the kingdom of Naples, once ruled by his ancestors, in southern Italy, and then to go on to recover the Holy Land. It was a great dream, and France was powerful enough to make it almost a reality.

Charles VIII was not an attractive person – he was a thick-witted man of 26 with a head physically too big for his stunted body; but he was king of the most powerful nation in Europe, and his big head was full of the old romances of chivalry, which he delighted in reading. The great glittering army of 40,000 that he led into the plains of Lombardy in September 1494 was fitted with the latest and best equipment of every kind. With him came his cousin Louis, duke of Orleans (four years later to succeed him on the throne as Louis XII), and most of the great nobles and ablest captains of France. Among the *gens d'armes* was a young squire whose friends called him Piquet and who would go on to become one of the greatest knights, Bayard. On the day this great army mustered at Asti to meet the king's ally, Ludovico Sforza, duke of Milan, far away in the chateau of Cognac a son was born to the count and countess of Angouleme. They called him Francis; and twenty years later he too would be leading a magnificent army into Italy, to win for a time the duchy of Milan, but only to lose it and his liberty at Pavia ten years later.

The royal house of France had a hereditary claim, though a thin one, to the crown of Naples, or the kingdom of the Two Sicilies as it was sometimes called. To press this claim a great invasion was planned. Charles' idea was to enter the north, secure in the shelter of his temporary alliance with Ludovico Sforza. Charles would then take his main army down through Italy. He would secure the Neapolitan kingdom, and then use it as a springboard to launch a great crusade to Palestine.

It was indeed a dream, and most of his advisers knew it was only a dream. But his ally, Ludovico Sforza, had something much more dangerous to worry about. He held the duchy of Milan because his great-grandfather had seized it from its rightful lords, the Visconti family; and Louis d'Orléans was descended from that family and had a better claim to the duchy than Sforza. So here we have Louis in Lombardy, a personage whose familial claims were threatening to Ludovico. And here we have Ludovico, uncertain of Louis d'Orléans' motives but realizing that a dream of conquest may have been in the mind of more than just Charles. Indeed, Louis d'Orléans had such a dream. In four years he would be king of France and duke of Milan, and Ludovico would be languishing as a prisoner in the grim French castle of Loches. After Louis came Francis, and after Francis died in 1547, his son, Henri, would persist in trying to hold onto Milan.

But those latter developments were all in the future. As for our present concerns, let's glimpse quickly at 1494, when Charles' army moved steadily down Italy unopposed, eventually taking the kingdom of Naples without a fight in February 1495. He had, as he thought, secured his lines of communication by his alliances with Savoy and Milan and by the neutrality of the Republic of Florence and the Papal States. What he had not reckoned with was the dismay and terror that his invasion had spread among all the states and cities of Italy. Within weeks of his seizing of Naples, the great powers of Italy – Milan, Venice, and the pope – had formed a league against him, with the support of the Emperor Maximilian and the Spanish king, Ferdinand of Castile and Aragon. A solemn treaty of alliance was signed in Venice on March 31, 1495.

The French army was not as strong as it had been, for large numbers had died, been killed by the local population, or had deserted. In addition, the army was completely cut off from its base in the north and from its homeland. Charles had a fleet in the Mediterranean, but it was not powerful enough to gain command of the sea from the fleets of Spain and Genoa.

Charles' invasion was the opening note of a terrible war-like nationalistic symphony that Europe has been playing ever since. It began a war – or rather a series of wars – for the conquest of Naples and of Milan that was to last, on and off, for two hundred years, and it was the seed from which every war in Europe up to World War II has sprung.

But the invasion was a godsend to the arms manufacturers of Italy and Germany. Under the pressure of necessity, the development of firearms progressed rapidly; but the art of the armorer had one last glorious fling before armor was made useless by the leaden balls of the arquebusier and musketeer. Indeed, during the first part of the wars (1495-1557), the production of weapons was prodigious.

Fifteenth-century armorers of Milan, Innsbruck, and Augsburg, but especially of Milan, had brought plate armor to a pitch of perfection that was never equalled. Not only was it effective as a defense; it achieved a beauty of line and proportion that marks off the armor of the period 1450-1510 from those of any other date. During those sixty years, the actual quality of the metal used, as well as the craftsmanship and often sheer artistry with which it was worked, surpassed any armor made before or after. The highest point was reached in the Milanese armor of the 1470s and 1480s; and it seems probable that conditions in Italy at that time created the demand for fine armor that spurred the designers and master-craftsmen on to such splendid efforts.

The history of Italy during the fifteenth century was one of continual rivalry among the numerous city-states, which were constantly at war with one another. These continual little wars created a need for fighting men that would only be satisfied by the development of highly organized, well-trained, and splendidly equipped mercenary bands. They were raised in the same manner that Richard I and King John raised hired crossbowmen – and, in the same way, the French and English Free Companies were raised during the Hundred Years' War and the German Landsknecht bands in the sixteenth century. A competent professional soldier, usually with one or two companions, would raise money and invest it in a band of fighting men. The more capital they raised, the bigger their force; and the more famous or popular a leader was, the more money he could obtain and the more men he could enlist. Such a leader was called a condottiere, and his company was a condotta. It was a company, too, in a somewhat modern sense: the condottiere was the managing director and his lieutenants were fellow directors. As for his men, they were his assets – and all his money was invested in them. You might think of them in modern terms as Malatesta Inc. or Bartolomeo Colleoni and Co. Ltd.

These condottieri were not crossbowmen or spearmen as in former times, but men-at-arms. Despite the successes of the English longbow in the French wars, in Italy and Germany the heavily armored cavalryman was the fighter with the highest prestige. This prestige contributed to the tremendous demand for first-class armor, but so, too, did the raising of large armies by the condottieri, where men-at-arms formed almost the entire force, with only a few crossbowmen or billmen (as spearmen were beginning to be called in the fifteenth century). Since it was costly to equip these mercenary men-at-arms, who demanded high rates of pay, the condottieri were reluctant to lose them in battle. The result was that all through the second half of the fifteenth century, Italian wars, fought by mercenary armies hired by rival princes or republics, became like elaborate games of oversized chess: two armies would maneuver until one had the other in a position from which it could be defeated – that is, if real fighting took place. Then the leaders on both sides would meet, look carefully at their respective powers and positions, and decide that A had defeated B. Then the A leader would remain where he was, in possession of the field, while B and his condotta would march away. It was a civilized and sensible way of waging war. Once in awhile, for the look of the thing, the two sides would put on a light skirmish; a man or two would be unhorsed, some armor would get dented, maybe a foot soldier or two would be killed; but it would be a disaster for a company if too much of its precious capital investment – its men – were killed or captured.

When Charles VIII led his magnificent army down the leg of Italy, the end had come for this style of "fighting." The French had been waging war, for real, for over two hundred years; they had no intention of playing the Italian game. Even when the great Italian powers of Milan, Venice, and the pope combined to oppose the French, they did not really appreciate the deadly intentions of the French leaders.

In a fierce fifteen-minute battle fought in a raging thunderstorm in a dry rocky valley in the

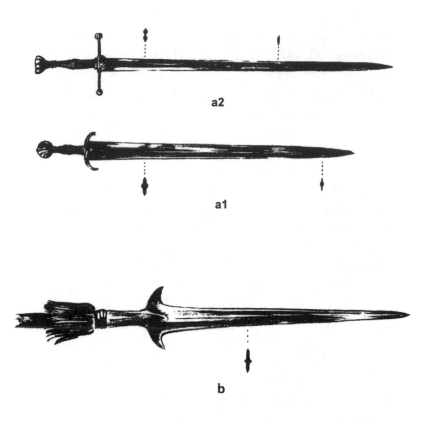

a2

a1

b

Arms in use at the time of Marignano: a. Knightly swords: a1, blade 31 inches long; a2, blade 37 inches long. b. Partisan – a big spearhead some 30 inches long with a 7-foot haft. The fighting ancestor of the ceremonial partisans still in use today, such as those carried by the Yeoman Warders at the Tower of London on state occasions. c. Pike-heads. d. Halberd head. The blade's edge is about 10 inches long; the spike at the top about 15 inches and the haft some 6 feet 6 inches. e. Bill. The entire head, with its variety of cutting edges, is some 30 inches long; the haft is 6 feet 7 inches long. f. Short swords (blades about 26 inches long) carried by mercenary infantry; f2, a Landsknecht sword (see illustration on page 15); and f1, a Swiss one.

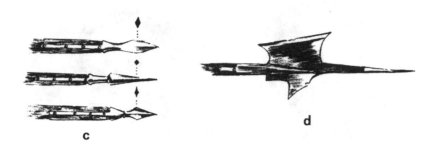

c

d

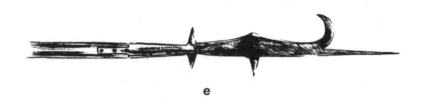

e

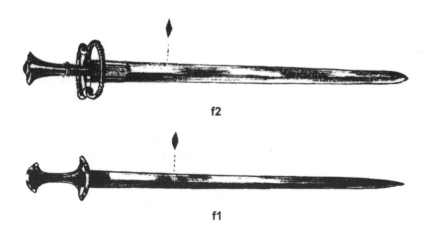

f2

f1

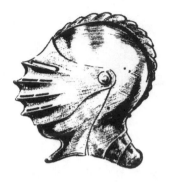

Helmets: on the left a "close-helmet" for a man-at-arms, on the right a light open helmet, worn by infantry officers or light cavalry.

Apennine mountains, Charles VIII's tired army, much reduced by a long and hasty march northward from Naples, soundly defeated a large, splendidly equipped force of Italian condottieri. Charles died soon after and was succeeded by his cousin, Louis d'Orléans, who turned his attention not so much to Naples as to his own ancestral domain of Milan – just as Ludovico Sforza had feared. For a time Louis gained Milan, but during the fifteen years of his reign the war raged throughout Italy and spread into Germany, becoming almost a world war for all the states of Europe; even the Turks in Asia were drawn into it. Milan changed hands again, and when, in 1515, Louis XII was succeeded by his young cousin, Francis I, it was held once more by a Sforza.

Francis was just twenty-one, a tall, intensely vital young man with a gleam in his eye and a fierce ambition to use his power to the utmost. To him, the dream of Milan became a crazy and terrible fantasy of conquest. The first thing he did was raise a great army, larger and better equipped than any his two predecessors had raised, and march it over a high Alpine pass down into the plains of northern Italy in a swift and sudden pounce that took his enemies completely off guard. Marching on toward the city of Milan itself, he halted some twelve miles away near the village of Marignano and at once began to negotiate with the Swiss allies of the duke of Milan, offering them an enormous bribe to desert.

Maximilian Sforza, a boy of sixteen, was completely in the power of a large force of Swiss, whose leaders formed a sort of committee that ran his duchy for him and whose hired fighting men comprised his only army. Francis was ready to fight, but he was prudent as well as ambitious, and his captains had fought the Swiss up and down Italy for the past twenty years. Nobody was going to be fool enough to fight them if they could be bought off instead.

So Francis started to negotiate, and the Swiss agreed to leave, for a price. They demanded 50,000 francs at once as down payment. Francis' army had been on the march for more than a month, and there were not even fifty francs in his pay-chests. He had no money, but his men did have some. He personally appealed to their generosity, then quickly made the rounds of the entire camp. He left his nobles with enough cash each to last a week, and skinned his common soldiers to the bone, but they loved him and paid up, maybe because they loved their own skins as well. He had his 50,000 francs by midday, and sent it off at once to the little town of Galarate

Francis I

under his veteran, Marshal Lautrec, with an escort, to
the Swiss committee of captains.

The Swiss accepted the deal. There were about
25,000 of them in all, and some 12,000 marched
home as soon as they got the money; the rest waited
until the following day. Francis may have been satisfied, but he had not taken into account the persuasive
tongue of Cardinal Mattias Schinner, a Swiss himself
and, far more important, an agent of the pope. In
1515 the pope was a great prince, one of the major
powers of Italy, and the last thing he wanted was to
see the king of France firmly seated in Milan. So at
the last minute, on the morning of September 15, the
cardinal went to work; even while the Swiss delegates
were counting their 50,000 francs in Galarate, some
seven miles from Milan, the Council of Captains met
in Milan itself. About half of them, those from Bern
and the western cantons of Switzerland, decided that
the agreement must be kept; so they marched their

men – some 12,000 pikes – away. But the cardinal persuaded the men from the eastern cantons to stay and fight. While the matter was still in the balance, the cardinal sent a body of Milanese on horse out of the city to drive off a French scouting party. The noise of this fight was heard inside the city, and Schinner persuaded the Swiss that they were being attacked. The alarm was sounded and all the remaining Swiss began hurriedly to muster in the great square in front of the cathedral. Schinner climbed on a chair that someone had put on the cathedral steps for him and made an emotional speech that soon set them howling for French blood. The Swiss then marched out of Milan, some 15,000 pikemen, twelve great cannon with their gunners, and a small force of about 200 Italian cavalry.

The French scouting force, led by Robert de la Marck, Sieur de Fleurange, one of Francis' captains, gave back before the advance of the pikemen, keeping in touch about a quarter of a mile ahead. For part of the way Cardinal Schinner rode up and down the Swiss line of march, talking and joking with the men and promising them an easy victory. When the leading column of the Swiss came near the French position, the long line of march was deployed into three great columns of men, about 5,000 in each. Then the front ranks lowered their pikes for the charge and moved forward again at a steady, fast walk.

Fleurange's cavalry was in danger of being nipped between a deep ditch and the advance of the leading column; there was no time to get across – the

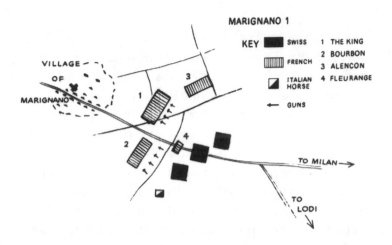

KEY

SWISS 1 THE KING
2 BOURBON
FRENCH 3 ALENCON
ITALIAN 4 FLEURANGE
HORSE

← GUNS

VILLAGE

OF

MARIGNANO

3

1

2

4

TO MILAN →

TO
LODI

only thing to do was to charge into the pikes and
hold the column up long enough to disengage and
cross the ditch. This didn't stop the Swiss, but it
slowed them; and although he lost many men and
horses, Fleurange got most of the force safely back
across the ditch. Then he rode with determined fury
to the king's tent.

Francis was certain the Swiss had deserted
Sforza, thus making a fight unnecessary. He was in
his tent trying on a beautiful new suit of armor when
Fleurange burst in, all dust and sweat, to tell him the
Swiss were attacking. Grabbing his sword, Francis
rushed out, yelling for his horse, and, amid the com-
motion and noise of his squadrons mounting their
horses, galloped forward to see what was going on.

Francis feared the Swiss, as well he should, but
there was no time to worry. Across the fields and
vineyards he could see a great cloud of grey dust rising, and heavy on the still air was a muffled rumbling

that became ever louder – the tramp of thousands of feet, the rattle and clink of arms as the Swiss approached grimly. Suddenly the Swiss war-horns bellowed their harsh, flat challenge, answered by the high ringing clamor of French trumpets. There was a thunderous roar of shouting and a grinding impact followed by a growing thunder of sound, a horrifying racket emanating from the clash of steel on steel, the roar of thousands upon thousands of voices yelling, singing, screaming; and below and behind the roar was the constant rumble of stamping feet.

The Swiss came on. Behind the ditch were fifteen French guns, and the vaward division of the duke of Bourbon. The guns got off a few shots before the Swiss pikemen came over the ditch to engage, pike against pike, with Bourbon's Landsknechts. This process – "push of pike" they used to call it – involved two blocks of pikemen simply pushing against each other, a bit like linemen in football going head to head. Most of the front-rank men on either side went down and then the two masses of stamping, slipping, pushing, cursing men came to a standstill. Slowly the Landsknechts gave ground; the Swiss overran the guns but got no farther. This column was halted by repeated charges from the French cavalry of the vaward division. Then the second Swiss column came up and clashed with the Landsknechts of the king's division in the center. Again the Landsknechts were pushed back, and again the great mass of pikemen was halted by repeated desperate charges of Francis' own squadrons.

It was getting dark. The battle had not started until about six in the evening, and the light was going. In the interval between his charges, the king and his captain of artillery, Galiot de Genouillac, got some of the guns to bear; the Swiss rushed desperately in but could not capture their foe, and they began to give back. As darkness fell, the battle's confusion was apparent. The three great columns of Swiss stayed in disciplined close formation – poised, bristling, and menacing – and only slowly moved back across the ditches; the French, meanwhile, charged in upon them whenever an opportunity came, brought on, in one sense, by the uncertain light of a rising moon.

During one of these moonlit encounters the chevalier, Pierre de Terrail, better known as Bayard (whose friends called him "Piquet," meaning Spur), had a strange, comical adventure that nearly cost him his life. His horse, wounded by several pike-thrusts, bolted and carried him right through a mass of Swiss, and would have carried him right into another if he hadn't been stopped by vine-trellises that he got tangled up in. Bayard managed to get off his horse and lie low for a few minutes trying to compose himself. Then he took off his helmet and leg harness and began to crawl on all fours along a ditch, toward a confused shouting that came among all the other shouts and groanings around him. The confused shouts sounded to him like "France, France!" He was right: it was the duke of Lorraine, hoarsely bawling the French battle-cry in an attempt to rally his scattered squadron. The duke was surprised to see the peerless Bayard in such a state – horseless and helmetless, drenched in water and covered with mud and duckweed. According to the account of Bayard's own man, who wrote his biography, the two knights had a good laugh; then the duke lent Bayard a splendid horse.

There is an intriguing tale about the horse, too. Bayard himself had captured it some years before during the siege of Brescia, and initially had given it to the duke of Lorraine. Its name was Le Carineau. At the battle of Ravenna in 1512 it had been terribly wounded – two pike-thrusts in its flanks and about twenty sword-cuts on its head. Bayard had imagined it was dead when it fell, but the next day, when the battlefield was being cleared, Le Carineau was found grazing peacefully. The horse was brought back to Bayard's quarters to heal. After that, whenever a sword caught Le Carineau's eye in a fight, he would rush forward and seize it with his teeth. It's been said that a more courageous horse has never been seen.

After Bayard got his horse back, he worried at having no helmet – not so much for protection from a physical blow but from an ailment: The heat in battle had warmed him, and, after being thoroughly soaked from his ordeal, he was scared of catching a cold with his head bare. But he borrowed the helmet of a friend, one of Lorraine's knights. Then Bayard returned to the battle.

For the moment all was quiet. Both sides were so worn out, and had become so scattered and mixed up, that a sort of peace was admitted, men throwing themselves down to rest among the butchered dead or clustering with their comrades, alert and wary, straining their eyes and ears in the dark mist to try to get some idea of where matters stood. The king had found a large gun, and for a while lay down on the trail of it, trying to get some sleep. He had been in the thick of the fighting all the time; his beautiful armor was battered, scratched, and blotched with ugly stains. Twice he had been knocked out, and one of the many pike-thrusts he had received went through his armor and the padded arming-doublet underneath. The king had been desperate with thirst, so his trumpeter had gone to one of the canals and brought some water. Francis couldn't see in the dark that it was mixed with blood. He drank it and it made him vomit. Even so, as he lay on his gun, sore and aching, crazy with thirst, he was happy. Nobody would ever call his knights "hares in armor" again (an appellation they received by running away at a battle at Guinegate in Flanders years before).

Francis didn't sleep this night. Just after midnight he saw fires glowing behind the Swiss columns. Was this to help the Swiss see in order to re-form their divisions? Or was it to cook food? Never mind: he got wearily to his feet and began prodding and kicking the tired artillerymen until they awoke. He couldn't find Genouillac, but it didn't matter. He went from gun to gun, telling the men to load and fire toward the tall clumps of pikes showing clearly against the glow of the fires. They got off a full volley. The Swiss hastily doused their fires and cleared out from the lighted spot after losing many men.

It turns out the fires had been lit to cook food, for Schinner and the duke of Milan had sent a great convoy of carts with provisions and tents for the wounded. Francis' cannonade had put a stop to the Swiss army's rest, though, and soon in the misty dark of the early morning, the great Swiss war-horns, the "Bull" of Uri and the "Cow" of Unterwalden, were bellowing their deep, flat calls to muster the pikemen into battle-order again. Soon the sharp notes of the French trumpets rang out to stir their men into action too.

During the hours before dawn, French commanders had re-formed the army into what was essentially one continuous line of battle. The duke of Bourbon's vaward division and the duke of Alencon's rearward had closed onto the flanks of the king's main-battle. As the light grew, the Swiss reconnaissance patrols saw and reported this new and far more formidable formation; but when the day saw light, the pikes came on again. "If they had charged fiercely overnight, they charged still more fiercely in the morning," wrote Fleurange in his account of the battle. The Swiss too had re-ordered their formation; instead of three large columns, they came on with two extra big ones and a smaller one. The largest, with the banner of Zurich at its head, came at the French center; the lesser one marched against Alencon on the left, while Bourbon on the right only had to face the small one. But this time Genouillac had his guns better placed, and had the range too.

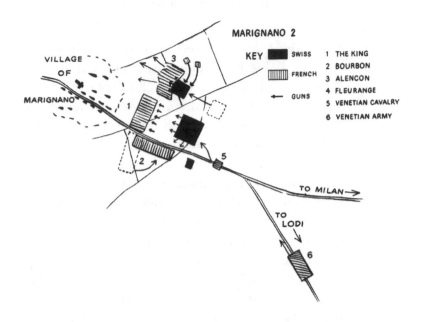

MARIGNANO 2

VILLAGE
OF
MARIGNANO

KEY   SWISS   1 THE KING
  FRENCH   2 BOURBON
  3 ALENCON
← GUNS   4 FLEURANGE
  5 VENETIAN CAVALRY
  6 VENETIAN ARMY

TO MILAN →

TO
LODI

Once those guns started moving, the main Swiss battle suffered terribly, but it came relentlessly on and
got to push of pike with the king's Landsknechts. But
while these fighters were preoccupied, Bourbon sent
in charges from the flank, and they had to form a
double front. This development brought them to a
standstill, with the guns still playing on them. One
desperate band made a heroic dash for the guns in an
attempt to stop the firing, but those men were cut
down. Only a single pikeman made it, and as he
clapped his hand on the nearest gun, he was struck
dead. Now Bourbon's charges began suffering very
badly.

The small column, facing Bourbon on the right
of the French line, stayed where it was and didn't risk
an attack, but on the left Alencon's division was

116

fiercely beset by the second Swiss "battle." The division made considerable headway, too, pushing the Landsknechts back a good deal. There were no guns in this division, and it was just a straightforward pikemen's fight. Some of the French troops broke and ran, spreading dismay in the rear of the line. The division was saved from disaster only by a series of brilliantly led cavalry charges by the squadrons under the Scottish soldier of fortune d'Aubigny (Robert Stuart, duke of Albany).

Things looked tricky on this side of the field. But in the center the French were completely successful, and the Swiss attack had failed. Now the Swiss began to doubt their chances of victory. "They saw that they had not as many men as they ought to have," wrote Fleurange.

The Swiss were in a nasty position. They had lost their impetus, and the whole column stood to be cut down by Genouillac's guns, and the repeated charges by the self-sacrificing French *gens d'armes* held them where they were. The Swiss could neither fight nor run. Their own guns, which they had placed on the road to harass the French center, had been knocked out as soon as it was light enough to see them.

The Swiss second column went on attacking the French left, but suddenly these attacks stopped too. A new force was coming up from behind. This was the Venetian light cavalry coming from Lodi. Bartolomeo d'Alviani, the Venetian general, had received Francis' message at the start of the battle the afternoon before. D'Alviani had ridden to Lodi to

Two knights of 1515. The one on our left is armed cap-á-pie (head to foot), and wears a long skirt, called "bares," over his armor. His horse wears a complete "bard" of plate armor. The one on the right is more lightly armed, for he wears only leather boots on his legs and a light open helmet. He has two swords, a long one on his left hip and a short one, rather like a Landsknecht sword, on his right. His horse, too, is lighter and has no "bard."

start his army off on the road to Marignano. His men had marched all through the night, and now at about 8 o'clock their leading squadrons were beating up the Swiss baggage guards, shouting "San Marco!" Great clouds of dust behind indicated that all 12,000 of the Venetian forces were poised for the fight.

So the day was lost to the Swiss. Sullenly they began to go back. It was a retreat that did the Swiss credit, perhaps more than any victory. There was no flight. In the most orderly way they picked up their wounded, collected their guns and baggage, and formed a rearguard to cover them. Then they marched off, back down the highway to Milan. The rearguard drove off the Venetian cavalry, killing its commander, Chiappino Orsini. This division of Swiss was driven into a village, and bottled up among the houses and battered by artillery until each man perished. A few other scattered parties of Swiss were cut up – one lot took refuge in a house and was burnt to death in it – but the main body went on to Milan. By midday it was over, just 24 hours since Schinner had promised the Swiss an easy victory.

"It was a marvel," wrote an Italian eyewitness, "to see the Swiss return to Milan – one had lost an arm, another a leg, a third was maimed by the cannon. They carried one another tenderly, and seemed like the sinners whom Dante pictured in the ninth circle of the *Inferno*. As fast as they came in they were directed to the hospital, which was filled in half an hour, and all the neighboring porches were strewn with straw for the wounded whom many Milanese, moved by compassion, tenderly succored."

Back on the field of battle, under the ruthless sun, lay the dead. Huge trenches were dug for them, and in the afternoon some 16,000 or 17,000 bodies were shoveled in. The French said there were two Swiss for each of their own combatants.

That evening at supper in his tent Francis was excitedly going over the tremendous events of the last two days; everyone was talking of the great deeds of arms that had been done. All agreed Bayard carried off the prize, as he generally did. Then this knight, known as the chevalier *sans peur et sans reproche* (without fear and without reproach), received a great honor from the king. Bayard's "loyal serviteur" has recounted the moment:

"Gentlemen, I have to bestow knighthood on some of you who have distinguished yourselves in this battle," the king said. "But I have never been knighted myself. Before I can knight anybody, I must receive the honor from one who is a knight; so Bayard, my friend, I want to have it from you."

"But, sir, a king, anointed by the oil from heaven, is surely a knight of knights?"

"Never mind. I want to be knighted by you, so hurry up and don't go into laws and canons. Do as I tell you!"

Bayard hesitated, and looked at the others. But he saw they all agreed with the king.

"Very well, sir, I can only obey." He drew his sword and said, "Sir, may this be as effective as if Roland, or Olivier, or Godfrey de Bouillon, or

Baldwin his brother, did it."

Francis knelt, and Bayard spoke the appointed words. As Francis got to his feet, Bayard smiled and said, "You're the first king I ever knighted!" Then he kissed his sword and lifted it and spoke to it.

"Most glorious sword! You are blessed to have given knighthood to so great a prince. Now you shall be honored as a relic, and I'll never use you again unless it's against the Infidel."

Then he sprang twice into the air, pointing his sword aloft, and returned it to the scabbard.

Just then Fleurange came in, still hot from pursuing the Swiss rearguard. Francis shouted for joy. "They told me you were dead!"

"Not by any means, sir. And I won't die so long as I can serve you!"

"Thank you, Fleurange. Now – I've just been knighted! I should be glad if you would accept knighthood from me!" So he knighted Fleurange and many others who had done well in the battle.

Francis' excitement over all this was intense; we can still feel it when we read the letter he sent to his mother the next day. He had been twenty-eight hours in the saddle, in his armor, without eating or drinking. He told her how he and his men had made twenty-five charges, and how he had been knocked out, and his armor pierced. "Not for 2,000 years has there been such a battle, one so ferocious and so cruel!" He praised the Swiss for their courage and discipline; mourned a bit for Humbercourt and De Bussy, both killed. And, at the end, he wrote: "Thank

God heartily, Madame, throughout the kingdom for the victory He has been pleased to give us. And, Madame, have a good laugh at this! Messiers Lautrec and Lescun missed the battle. They were kept negotiating with the Swiss, and the Swiss were pulling their legs!"

This letter survives. So too does much more of the material stuff with which history is made. In the armories at the Tower of London is an armor of Bayard's. Fleurange's armor is in the Kunsthistorisches Museum in Vienna. In the Metropolitan Museum of Art in New York is a splendid armor, made in Henry VIII's royal armory at Greenwich a few years after Marignano, for Galiot de Genouillac. And in the Musee de l'Armee in Paris is a splendid, slender armor 6 feet 4 inches tall that once enclosed Francis' long form. In Windsor Castle is a shield once belonging to Bayard, which he gave to England's King Henry VIII. A sword, believed to be the one Bayard used to knight his king, used to be in an English private collection, but the whereabouts of this sword have since become unknown.

Those things that we still have from medieval fighting days certainly help to bring vividly to life the actual people we read about. Nothing, not even a good portrait, can so clearly bring before our eyes the very form, stance, and person of the owner of a piece of armor or a weapon. I have written elsewhere of the armors of Henry VIII, how it takes very little imagination to feel that each of them still encloses the flesh and blood of that most royal person. So, too, in

Francis' armor we can see the man in it. The one in the Musee de l'Armee was made for him several years after Marignano, but there he is – tall, long elegant legs, a bit of a paunch, broad strong shoulders, and an upright carriage. We can, if we try, almost see the twinkle of a bright brown eye through the eye-slit of his visor, and, across the centuries, a chuckle echoes inside the bever.

Of all the surviving hardware of these personages, only Fleurange's armor might have been worn at Marignano: it is of superb quality, plain, unadorned, the workaday field harness of the professional fighting man that he was; the surviving armor of the others comes from later dates. But those were, to be sure, the men.

Postscript

We have looked in some detail at four battles fought between the end of the twelfth century and the beginning of the sixteenth – four out of the hundreds of big battles and the countless small engagements involving knights during those centuries. We have seen how the forces on one side or the other – and at Marignano on both sides – fought with a firm discipline that we tend to think is only a fairly modern approach. In the popular mindset, it is still often believed that medieval armies were unskilled and riotous mobs of brutal and undisciplined soldiery, led by men ignorant of the finer points of tactics or strategy. Like most popular beliefs, this is nonsense.

Many of these battles so remote from our own time were in fact very similar to more recent ones. In the great battle in the marshy estuary of the river Garigliano in southern Italy, fought in bitter wet weather over Christmas 1502, conditions and tactics were very similar to those used at the Somme in 1916 – trenches, artillery barrages, snipers, mud and all.

(This battle in 1502 is the one in which Louis XII's army was destroyed in his attempt to conquer the kingdom of Naples.) A fierce little fight outside Jaffa in 1192, on the other hand, has many parallels to fights between American Indians and the army in the American West in the 1870s, and with similar, though larger, engagements in the Sudan in the 1880s.

After his victory at Arsuf, King Richard went on to the port of Jaffa and refortified it. Leaving a garrison, he took his main force on toward Jerusalem, but he never got there. The armies of Saladin were too strong for the Crusaders to be able to lay siege to the Holy City, so Richard had to turn back. There is a fine romantic tale of how, when he had taken the hard decision to retreat, Richard went with some of his knights to the top of a hill to reconnoiter the land he would have to pass on his way back to Acre. One of his knights, who knew the country well, called to Richard: "Sir, if you look over here you can see Jerusalem!" The king twitched his shield round from his back and held it in front of his face. "If I may not take it, I am not worthy to look at it," he said, and turned his horse away.

We shall never know if this story is apocryphal, but it is in keeping with what we do know of this remarkable man's character, and with the spirit of the age he lived in. We do know, as well, that the story of the battle at Jaffa on August 5, 1192, is true enough.

After Richard had returned to Acre, Saladin had come down to the coast in force to recapture Jaffa. By late July the garrison had evacuated the newly fortified town and retreated into the castle, and was about to surrender when Richard suddenly appeared off the harbor. He had come down the coast with every ship that was ready for sea. There were only eight available, and he had packed each tiny craft full, with as many fighting men as it could hold. Even so, he only had fifty-five knights, fifteen horses, and some two thousand spearmen and crossbowmen. With this little force, and the garrison, he drove the Saracens out of town on August 1. But when Saladin heard how few men his adversary had, he swooped down with a large force of his heavy-armed cavalry, mostly Mamelukes and Kurds. He came in the dark of the night of August 4, hoping to overwhelm the crusader's camp outside Jaffa while they slept; but Richard was warned in time. Rousing his men, he rapidly formed them in battle order, in a square or a circle. He put his spearmen in the first rank, every man kneeling on one knee with his spear held at an angle in front of him, the point on a level with a horse's breast and the end firmly secured against his foot – just as the men of the Black Watch held their bayoneted rifles at the battle of El Teb in 1884. Behind stood the crossbowmen, one in each interval between two spearmen. It was this soldier's job to shoot as fast as possible the loaded crossbows handed to him by another who stood behind him, bending and loading each empty one as it was passed back. In this way it was possible to keep up a continuous fire on the enemy.

The Saracens swept down, wave after wave, but never dared close the bristling hedge of spears. Every squadron turned and swept by; their arrows did little harm, but they suffered much from the bolts of the Christians. When they were in disorder, Richard charged out with his fifteen mounted knights, cutting deep into the mass of the Saracens and then turning and cutting a way out, rescuing two knights – the earl of Leicester and Sir Ralph de Mauleon – who had been surrounded.

The fight lingered on for some hours, but the square held firm and the surprise had failed. After some time every man who could be spared from the ships came ashore and joined in, and the Saracens gave up the fight and fled. They left several hundred dead men and more than a thousand horses on the sand. Only two Franks fell, so closely had the square been held.

There were many battles fought just like that, even as recent as the 1880s, when English soldiers faced ferocious, incredibly brave Muslim warriors armed like their ancestors with spear and round shield and long straight two-edged sword. Instead of men-at-arms there were the officers and men of the Tenth and Nineteenth Hussars, who fought with swords in the same way as their ancestors had seven hundred years before; and instead of spears, the infantrymen used bayonets and rifles. But the battles in the Sudan in the 1880s were scarcely any different from battles the crusaders fought in the deserts of Palestine and Jordan.

Sudanese attack on a British square at Tamar in 1884, during the Sudanese Rebellion.

Until the appearance of weapons of mass destruction, all battles had points in common, whether they were fought by Greeks or Romans, medieval knights, the Troopers of Cromwell or Wallenstein, or the men of Marlborough or Wellington. In the Crimea and the Sudan, in South Africa and even on the Marne in 1914, some of the ancient arms and tactics were used. But now, with nuclear weapons holding a sort of desperate balance, we have, in a perhaps ironic way, returned to those days of fifteenth-century Italy before the French came, when the "material" of armies was far too precious and expensive to risk in the perilous uncertainty of battle.

Glossary

Abergavenny Castle – erected in Wales by eleventh-century Normans. The town around the castle was often attacked.

Agincourt – the Battle of Agincourt took place on Oct. 25, 1415, in the midst of the Hundred Years' War between France and England. At Agincourt (in France), Henry V of England led his army to victory over the French, who suffered terrible losses, including the death of constable Charles I d'Albert, a dozen high-ranking nobles, and thousands of other knights and men-at-arms. The English losses were slight.

Angevin – pertaining to the Plantagenets, an English family line that ruled from the mid-twelfth century until the late fourteenth. The Black Prince (see below) was a Plantagenet.

Apennines – mountain range in Italy that stretches from north to south across the western part of the peninsula.

Arbalestier – one who uses an arbalest, a medieval crossbow.

Arquebusier – one who wields a portable firearm known as an arquebus. Now obsolete, it is also referred to as a harquebus.

Augsburg – city in Bavaria in southwest Germany.

Baldwin I – king of Jerusalem who lived from 1058 to 1118. He was the brother of Godfrey de Bouillon (see below).

Bannockburn – village in Scotland near Stirling. Name of decisive battle in which Robert Bruce, King of Scots, beat England's Edward II in 1314.

Barded horses – horses covered with fabric or armor.

Barons' War – from 1263 until 1267; a civil war in England in which barons revolted against the incompetent and fiscally destructive leadership of Henry III. In 1266 a settlement was reached, but it wasn't until 1267 that some of the barons' chief complaints were resolved.

Bascinet – a spherical-shaped or pointed helmet, usually with a visor. Also spelled "basinet."

Battle of El Teb – waged in the Sudan (see below) against the British army in 1884.

Battle of Lewes – a fight in the midst of the Barons' War in England. It was the battle at which the barons captured Henry III and seized power in May 1264.

Bayard, a.k.a. Pierre de Terrail – a French knight born in 1473. Known for fearlessness and bravery, he was considered by many to be the ideal knight. His friends called him Piquet, meaning Spur.

Bedouin – Arab wanderer of the Syrian, Arabian, African, or Asian deserts.

Billman – what a spearman was beginning to be called in the fifteenth century.

Birket-el-Ramadan – a large marsh that protected the Crusaders on one side as they rested at the Nahr-el-Falaik in between attacks by Saladin.

Black Prince – Edward Plantagenet, Prince of Wales, a great commander whose fiery genius helped the English defeat France at Poitiers in 1356, perhaps the best-fought battle by the English during the Hundred Years' War against France.

Black Watch – a unit of Scottish foot soldiers in the British military.

Boha-ed-Din – Saracen chronicler of events during the Crusades, he offers a vivid account of the organized marching and tough demeanor of the Christian foe during the battle of Arsuf in 1191.

131

Boer War – war from 1899–1902 pitting England against the Transvaal and Orange Free State, provinces in South Africa. Also name of war in 1880-81 between Great Britain and the Transvaal.

Brest – seaport in northwest France in Britanny.

Breton – one who lives in Brittany; also refers to the particular Celtic language of the people of Brittany.

Bridgehead – an area around or near a bridge that has been strengthened, especially to afford defensive protection from an enemy's offensive onslaught; also a position secured within a foe's area that is used to further one's advance.

"Bull" of Uri – a great war horn.

Canton – small territory within a country, especially a division within Switzerland.

Carentan – town in northwest France.

Castellan – the person who runs or governs a castle.

Cat – a nickname for the large, moveable shed, covered with animal hides and sometimes sheets of iron, used to house and protect the various rams, picks, and bores and the men who worked them during a siege.

Cinque Ports – group of maritime towns in Sussex and Kent in England. In exchange for helping with the country's sea defense, they were granted certain benefits. Their help was needed after the regent's victory at Lincoln Fair in 1217 when French reinforcements continued a fighting campaign. The seamen of Cinque Ports rallied to the royal cause, and, in a great sea battle off the coast of Dover on August 25, they helped defeat the French soundly.

Colleoni, Bartolomeo – a fifteenth-century military entrepreneur in Italy; he tried to establish a state in northern Italy in 1467 but was eventually stopped.

Condottiere – a leader of mercenary armies in Italy, especially in the fourteenth and fifteenth centuries.

Courser – a swift-moving, spirited horse.

"Cow" of Unterwalden – a great war horn.

Count de la Perche – leader of the French contingent who fancied himself the leader of the entire rebels' army that went against the regent of England, William Marshal, at the battle of Lincoln in 1217.

Courtrai – city in northwest Belgium.

Crécy – in northern France, site of 1346 battle won by England mostly by archers and their terrible weapon in the early part of the Hundred Years' War.

Crimea – area in the southern Ukraine alongside the Crimean Peninsula.

Cromwell, Oliver – born April 25, 1599 and died Sept. 3, 1658; he led parliamentary forces in the English Civil Wars of the seventeenth century.

Crossbow – many types have been developed, but essentially it is a weapon with a bow fixed crosswise on a wooden stock. A soldier armed with one was called a crossbowman.

Crusades – a number of Christian military pilgrimages and battles waged against Muslim influence in the Holy Land. They lasted from the late eleventh century until the late thirteenth century.

De Bouillon, Godfrey – lived roughly from 1061 to 1100. French leader of the Crusades around whom many legends have grown.

De Lusignan, Guy – king of Jerusalem from 1186-1187; descendant of old powerful family in Poitou in France. Was captured by Saladin in 1187 and set free a year later upon giving up any claim to the kingship. Supported by Richard I at siege of Acre. Richard I bestowed upon him the title king of Cyprus in 1192

De Montfort, Simon – led English revolt in which barons opposed Henry III, capturing him at the Battle of Lewes in May

1264. De Montfort had primary power in the country from then until his death in August 1265.

Duchy – territory of a duke or duchess.

Du Guesclin, Bertrand – known as "the Eagle of Brittany," he was born circa 1320 and died 1380. Instrumental in pushing English out of parts of France. Served country well under kings John II and Charles V and became a count in 1364. Captured by Edward, Black Prince of Wales, in 1367 but then was set free for a fee. Was made duke of Molinas in 1369 and constable of France in 1370.

Dupplin Moor – site of 1332 battle in which Scotland suffered a terrible defeat at the hands of the English.

Eleanor of Aquitaine – born probably in 1122 and died in 1204. She was queen to Louis VII of France but then divorced. She married Henry of Anjou, who became King Henry II of England, thus putting in motion conflicts and entanglements between France and England that would persist for hundreds of years.

Emir – an Arab prince; ruler, especially in parts of Asia and Africa.

Esquire – a person of the British gentry just below a knight's station; one vying to become a knight who attends to a knight.

Foot-sergeant – the professional infantry in a medieval army. Compared to men-at-arms, foot-sergeants were lightly armed, with their chief weapon being a spear about six feet long.

Franks – during the time of the Crusades, the Saracens referred to all people of Europe as "Franks," so this is the name they gave to their Christian foes.

Gambeson – garment worn under hauberk. (see below)

Garrison – defenders stationed at a castle.

Gens d'armes – French phrase for men-at-arms (see below), from which is derived the current word "gendarme," meaning an armed policeman entrusted with keeping civil order.

Giaour – Turkish word meaning a nonbeliever or non-Muslim; it was used often by Muslims during the Crusades to refer to Christians.

Grimsby – in east England in Lincolnshire.

Halberd – a weapon with a broad, short blade on a five-foot haft; it emerged from the marriage of the bill-hook and spear.

Halidon Hill – fourteenth-century battle on the Scottish border won by the English.

Hauberk – tunic or coat, made of leather or of mail, that served as defensive protection for a warrior.

Holy Land – Palestine, known in the Bible as Canaan, on the east coast of the Mediterranean. Now divided between Israel and the state of Jordan.

Homines ad armas – Latin phrase for men-at-arms (see below).

Hobelar – an unarmored horseman in the Middle Ages, a kind of medieval dispatch-rider.

Hospitaller – member of a religious military order founded around 1096-1099.

Hundred Years' War – series of wars from 1337 until 1453 pitting England against France. The Hundred Years' War essentially began because Edward III was obsessed with his grandfather's dream of uniting England and Scotland. Edward III realized that, since the French often helped the Scots, he would have to fight the French first if he wanted to incorporate Scotland under the English crown.

Infidel – someone without religious faith. Both the Christians and the Muslims disparagingly called each other "infidels" during the time of the Crusades.

Innsbruck – city in what is now Austria.

Itinerarium Regis Ricardi – known also as The Operations of King Richard, it provides a descriptive firsthand account from the Christian perspective of the Saracens' attacks.

Joan of Arc – known as the Maid of Orléans, she lived from 1412 to 1431. France's national heroine, she believed angels' voices, or perhaps God's, directed her initially to lead a pious life and then to guide France during turbulent times. She led an army that forced the English to retreat from siege of Orléans.

Keep – the strongest, most secure tower of a castle

Knight-errant – a wandering knight, one who did not swear permanent allegiance to a lord; instead, the knight errant traveled around, seeking adventure wherever he could find it.

Knollys, Sir Robert – Englishman who, as one of Edward III's captains of Free Companies, made a name for himself up and down France in the fourteenth century. He would become known by the French as "Robert le Terrible," for when it came to fighting, he was terrible indeed.

Kurds – ethnic group living mainly in Iran, Iraq, and Turkey. Saladin was a Kurd.

Le Carineau – name of the horse of the great knight Bayard (see above). It was wounded badly at the battle of Ravenna in 1512 and presumed dead. But the next day, Le Carineau was found grazing peacefully. It was brought to Bayard to heal, and, from then on, Le Carineau gained a reputation as the most dependable, courageous horse around.

Legate – an emissary functioning in an official capacity.

Lincoln Fair – The Battle of Lincoln in 1217 brought so much plunder or spoils to the army of regent William Marshal that it became known as Lincoln Fair, which has been its name ever since.

Lombardy – region in northern Italy.

Longbow – the archer's weapon; the great distance and accuracy with which it could launch penetrating arrows helped lead to complete, close-fitting armor.

Lynn – town in England that held out for King John as late as

October 1216, even after the signing of the Magna Carta in 1215 (see below). The town, in eastern England, has been King's Lynn ever since.

Magna Carta – the Great Charter, which rebel barons forced King John to sign in 1215 at Runnymede. It granted them certain liberties, but they began acting as if they ruled the land, while the king had no real intention of surrendering his power.

Mail – armor that was flexible, consisting of rings linked together or of small exterior plates.

Malatesta – Italian family from Rimini that played a significant role in the country's affairs from the thirteenth to the sixteenth centuries. Sigismondo Pandolfo, a family member, was a skilled soldier who warred against the pope and was excommunicated from the church in 1460.

Mamelukes – slaves forced into military service; they gained power in many Muslim areas in the Middle Ages. Also spelled "Mamluks."

Meinie – group of followers or dependents; retinue. Also spelled "meiny."

Men-at-arms – called *gens d'armes* by the French, they were the heavy cavalry of a fighting unit. They fought with lance and sword, were armored in mail from head to foot, and rode "barded" and "covered" horses. They were of two types: knights and sergeants. In a medieval army, knights were officers and sergeants were troopers.

Musketeer – one wielding a musket, a handgun first used in the sixteenth century that was a precursor to more sophisticated rifles.

Nahr-el-Falaik – between this river-mouth, called the River of Caesarea by Boha-ed-Din, and the ruined town of Arsuf, Saladin had planned a desperate attack in order to keep the Christians from getting to Jaffa, a former city and port in what is now Israel. Since 1950 it has been a section of Tel Aviv. The Nahr-el-Falaik was a spot where the Crusaders rested.

Naker – a kettledrum

Olivier – friend of Roland (see below). Legend paints him as possessing a more level-headed courage than Roland's fiery demeanor.

Page – a boy in training to be a knight.

Paris, Matthew – English historian of medieval period, he lived from 1200 to 1259.

Paynim – during the time of the Crusades, Christians often referred to Muslim Arabs contemptuously as the "foul Paynim," while Muslims referred to the Crusaders as "Christian dogs," among other names.

Philip Augustus – Philip II of France, one of Europe's leading rulers and perhaps the most efficient French king during the Middle Ages. Because of his growing power and statesmanship, he became known as Philip Augustus, a reference to Roman leader Augustus Caesar, who ruled from 27 B.C. until A.D. 14.

Pikeman – a professional, non-noble, peasant soldier who fought unarmored in disciplined massed companies, with only the officers and front-rank men wearing light half-armor. As one might guess, pikemen fought with pikes, spears some 15 feet to 18 feet long.

Piquet – name given to the great knight Bayard by his friends. It means Spur.

Postern – an entranceway on the side or out of view that is not for general access; a gate in the back.

Regent – one who exercises authority in a kingdom; someone who oversees the governance of an area in the absence of the acknowledged ruler.

Roland – hero in many medieval poems and legends.

Roman Empire – dominant world power whose empire was established in 27 B.C. and lasted in the West until roughly the fifth century A.D.

Routiers – the name ordinary folk usually gave to professional crossbowmen. It means "highwaymen," and that's basically what most of these men were: highway robbers turned professional soldiers. They were hated and despised.

Royal standard – banner of the king, serving as a rallying point or emblem.

Saint George – patron saint of England and a Christian martyr about whom little is known with certainty. He probably lived in the third century, though he was not known in England until the eighth.

Saracen – a nomadic Arab. Often referred to Muslims who were engaged in that grueling war with Christians known as the Crusades, fought in the eleventh, twelfth and thirteenth centuries.

Sforza, Ludovico – lived from 1451 to 1508. Known as "the Moor," he was duke of Milan from 1481 to 1499. He would be defeated by Louis XII and languish as a prisoner in the grim French castle of Loches.

Sieur – once used as a title of rank or to show respect for someone; it is now confined mainly to legal use.

Sleaford – in eastern part of England.

Squire – a candidate for knighthood who serves as an attendant for a knight.

Sudan – largest country in Africa, located in the northeast part of the continent. General Charles Gordon, a European Christian, was named governor-general of the Sudan in 1877. His efforts to crush the slave trade ultimately backfired. Hoodwinked perhaps by his Christian status in a Muslim area, he underestimated the blow to the Sudanese economy brought on by his campaign. The Sudanese themselves generally came to view his crusade as a Christian movement antithetical to Islamic precepts. Gordon had to resign. The Sudan, in turmoil, eventually was controlled in June 1881 by Muhammad Ahmad, who anointed himself the Mahdi, meaning a messiah picked by Allah. After the Mahdists had demolished an Egyptian army in late 1883, Gordon was dispatched to Khartoum, the capital city of Sudan, in 1884. He needed help, but before the British arrived, the city was taken and Gordon beheaded.

Tamar – site of insurrection in the Sudan (see above) against the British army in the1880s.

Templar – a professional soldier-monk whose religious military order was founded by the Crusaders around 1118 and squelched in 1312. The order came about to protect Christian pilgrims and the Holy Sepulcher.

Tiberias – city on western shore of Sea of Galilee.

Turcopoles – lightly armored horsemen on the Christian side who fought with bows in the Saracen manner.

Van – troops at the front of a military unit, derived from the word "vanguard."

Varlet – a knight's attendant or page; a person of low rank.

Wallenstein – born in 1583. Austrian general who lost estates in the Thirty Years' War, which lasted from 1618 until 1648 and eventually involved German Protestants and Catholics, plus France, Sweden, Denmark, Spain and the Holy Roman Empire. He was murdered in 1634.

War of the Roses – struggles in England from 1455 until 1485 between the House of Lancaster and the House of York for control of the monarchy.

Wulfstan – high-ranking English ecclesiastic, made a saint in 1203. Lived in the eleventh century.

INDEX